When the War
Never Ends

When the War Never Ends

The Voices of Military Members with PTSD and Their Families

LEAH WIZELMAN

ROWMAN & LITTLEFIELD PUBLISHERS, INC.

Lanham • Boulder • New York • Toronto • Plymouth, UK

Published by Rowman & Littlefield Publishers, Inc.
A wholly owned subsidiary of The Rowman & Littlefield Publishing Group, Inc.
4501 Forbes Boulevard, Suite 200, Lanham, Maryland 20706
http://www.rowmanlittlefield.com

Estover Road, Plymouth PL6 7PY, United Kingdom

British Library Cataloguing in Publication Information Available

Library of Congress Cataloging-in-Publication Data
Wizelman, Leah.
  [Wenn der Krieg nicht endet. English]
  When the war never ends : the voices of military members with PTSD and
their families / Leah Wizelman.
    p. cm.
  Summary: "Service members returning from deployment are often suffering
from PTSD. Its symptoms include distressing flashbacks, memories and
nightmares, aggression, memory problems, physical symptoms, loss of positive
emotions, and withdrawal from society. *When the War Never Ends* tells the
stories of those who have lived it themselves–affected veterans and active-
duty personnel, as well as their spouses, from the U.S., Canada, Australia,
and Germany, who were participants in various wars and peace missions.
The stories will help family members better understand their loved ones by
vividly demonstrating what a trauma survivor is feeling and going through"—
Provided by publisher.
    ISBN 978-1-4422-1207-7 (hardback) — ISBN 978-1-4422-1209-1
(electronic)
    1. Post-traumatic stress disorder. 2. War—Psychological aspects. 3.
Soldiers—Mental health. 4. Soldiers—Interviews. 5. Families of military
personnel—Interviews. I. Title.
  RC552.P67W5913 2010
  616.85'212—dc23   2011020662

∞™ The paper used in this publication meets the minimum requirements
of American National Standard for Information Sciences—Permanence of
Paper for Printed Library Materials, ANSI/NISO Z39.48-1992.

Printed in the United States of America

I dedicate this book to my interview partners, listed in the order of their stories:
J. D. B., J. C. W., Canadian Corporal, Hauptfeldwebel Frank, Ex-Staff Sergeant Michael, Peter, Cathy, Chief Petty Officer Second Class CD2 Retd. P., Sergeant Doyle, S. S., Andrew, D. R., Björn, Specialist A. L., Warrant Officer André, Bunnie, Private R., Allison, Pat, Chief Hospital Corpsman Gordon, Oberfeldwebel S. H., P. S., Sergeant Dave, Stabsunteroffizier Christian, Jamal, Vince, Sergeant Marcus, Stephanie, Lana, Former Acting Sub-Lieutenant John, Friedhelm, Sergeant Pierre

Contents

CONTENTS

Foreword

While dedicating the Boston Medical Library in 1901, Sir William Osler pointed out that "to study the phenomena of disease without books is to sail an uncharted sea, while to study books without patients is not to go to sea at all." This same logic led Osler to insist that medical students learn at their patient's bedside rather than spend their entire education in lecture halls. He also invented the modern residency training system, which brought new doctors into daily interaction with patients by quite literally making them residents of the hospital. These innovations became standard in medical training worldwide.

In writing *When the War Never Ends: The Voices of Military Members with PTSD and Their Families*, Leah Wizelman follows Osler's example by reclaiming the subject of traumatic stress from the *Diagnostic and Statistical Manual of Mental Disorders* (*DSM*) of the American Psychiatric Association and countless other texts and research journals (as well as the hearing rooms of myriad disability claims programs) and insisting that we learn about it directly from people who actually live with it. This is altogether fitting because it is exactly the way in which the concept of psychological trauma and of posttraumatic stress disorder (PTSD) came to medical attention in the first place.

In 1980, as a Yale psychiatry resident at the West Haven Veterans Affairs (VA) Medical Center, I met many veterans who would eventually be diagnosed with PTSD but that diagnosis had not yet been published in the *DSM*. PTSD became an official mental disorder with the release of the *DSM-III* later that year, but there is another honored tradition in medical education that delayed my use of the term until the very end of my training: doctors learn to formulate diagnoses from their teachers rather than from their textbooks. I first used the term PTSD three years later—and only after I heard my former VA ward chief give a lecture on it.

Resident physicians are constantly called on to make decisions they have never made before, and even the most innocuous of these feels suffused with responsibility for the patient's life or death. For example, one of our first clinical psychotherapy seminars ended with a senior psychiatrist's suggestion that we new residents avoid doing psychotherapy for the first few weeks and instead "just talk with the patients." I can remember my relief when, a few days later, I found out that I wasn't the only one of my classmates living in frank dread that, while "just talking" with a patient, I might accidentally "do psychotherapy." Even "just talking" with patients feels dangerous to new doctors who cannot yet count on their own experience or find "the right answers" in their medical texts.

Wizelman therefore seems either brave or brazen in suggesting that we "just read" what service members, veterans, and their family members have to say. Isn't PTSD the province of mental health professionals? The answer must be a resounding "No!" As readers will find, PTSD and related posttraumatic problems properly belong to those who live with them rather than those who treat them. It was, in fact, people living with such problems (you couldn't even call them patients since most were not in treatment at the time) who first made the medical establishment aware of the need to coin the phrase posttraumatic stress disorder.

It wasn't easy for PTSD to gain official recognition from the American Psychiatric Association, and the process didn't begin in the laboratory or even in the clinic. Clinicians had long been aware of deployment-related diagnoses such as "effort syndrome" in the American Civil War, "shell shock" in World War I, and "battle fatigue" in World War II, but interest in them waned with the end of each successive conflict. During the Vietnam War, military medical leaders congratulated themselves that rigorous application of battlefield principles learned in previous wars had successfully stemmed the number of psychiatric casualties in combat. On the other hand, concerns began to be raised by Vietnam veterans that something was going wrong among many of them who had already come home. Having been either ignored or rebuffed by the medical establishment, Vietnam veterans self-organized into rap groups where they found personal dignity and therapeutic value in sharing the kind of testimony that Wizelman shares with us in this volume. These conversations were, in those days, reserved for fellow veterans who would doubt neither their integrity nor their sanity.

The long and difficult translation of intimate narratives into a scientifically validated, officially sanctioned diagnostic entity began when some of these veterans invited psychiatrists like Chaim

Shatan and Robert J. Lifton into their rap groups. These medical men faced no easy struggle in getting their colleagues to share their conviction that there was, indeed, a post-Vietnam stress syndrome that would eventually be called PTSD. Nor was there quick acceptance that PTSD might also apply to other survivor groups. For example, in its first years, the concept of PTSD remained so closely tied to the specific stressors of Vietnam that most clinicians did not recognize that rape survivors also met full criteria for PTSD. It was well into the 1980s that VA clinicians began routinely asking World War II and Korean War veterans who they had been treating for years about PTSD symptoms. As a result, we will never know the full psychiatric consequences of those wars.

The great irony of my career is that I trained at a time when virtually no one expected PTSD, and I now approach retirement at a time when virtually everyone, professional and layperson alike, has heard of PTSD and seems to expect that every veteran comes home from war with it. The odds of getting PTSD are probably somewhere in between. Every veteran described in this book has met full diagnostic criteria for PTSD, but their reports and those of their family members can't be completely reduced to this label even though it is clinically accurate and useful. Many other people and their families also struggle daily with profound and persistent problems as a consequence of psychological trauma whether or not they meet full diagnostic criteria. As you read this book, I advise you to pause before framing any of these reports in clinical terms. They deserve to first be heard as human stories.

Medical science and clinical technique achieve daily progress in characterizing PTSD. Clinical practice guidelines now lead professionals from accurate assessment to effective, evidence-based psychotherapeutic and psychopharmacologic treatment of PTSD. Major systems of care, including the U.S. Department of Veterans Affairs and the British, Australian, and Canadian national health systems, have adopted systematic PTSD screening and referral programs. Regardless, one of the most important lessons to be learned about PTSD is that its manifestations and effects on military men and women, veterans, and their families cannot be sequestered in textbooks, algorithm, or even clinics. My thanks to Leah Wizelman for enabling so many to tell profound human stories in profoundly human terms. As Osler would remind us, to understand the psychological aftermath of war, we must listen to the warriors and those who share their burdens. Until we do, despite our best professional efforts to understand PTSD, we will be no more fit for our own purpose than are sailors who have never gone to sea at all.

Harold Kudler, MD, Associate Clinical Professor,
Duke University Medical Center, February 2011

Preface

Several years ago, I happened to hear about U.S. troop support programs that put civilians in contact with deployed service members. The idea was to recognize their efforts and help brighten their days through supportive mail and care packages. It felt like a worthy thing to do, and I decided to participate. That's how I got in touch with military members in Iraq and Afghanistan.

It was the first time that I was directly confronted with the life and job of servicemen and women. Suddenly, the war was brought right into my home. Now, I was personally getting to know people who took part in dangerous missions and experienced horrible events. I started to occupy myself with the psychological consequences of deployments and developed a special interest in combat- and military-related posttraumatic stress disorder (PTSD).

Reading a list of PTSD symptoms cannot even come close to conveying what it really feels like to suffer from PTSD, not to mention the effect it has on family members. I discovered that learning firsthand these men's and women's personal stories was indeed the most memorable way to learn about PTSD. I decided to write a book that portrays touching stories of current and former service members with PTSD and their families and to let readers experience PTSD through the eyes of those affected. As a biologist involved in research on mechanisms of stress regulation in PTSD patients, I have the necessary background knowledge in this area.

I recruited my interview partners from the Internet or found them through organizations, and since this began, I have been deeply touched by the trust they have shown to me, a stranger. Some have confessed that it has helped them just to be able to talk to me, and this means a lot to me. I hope this book will further help them, as well as others in the same situation.

If you are an affected person, I hope that my book will help you by showing you that you are not alone in your suffering, that you are neither "crazy" nor a "wimp," but that you do have a known disorder.

If you are family or a friend, I hope that these stories will vividly demonstrate to you what a service member with PTSD is experiencing and thus lead to a better understanding. I hope it will give you strength and patience to cope with the inter-personal problems that can be caused by PTSD. Reading how others in the same situation deal with them may also be helpful.

If you are a student, I hope these powerful personal accounts will help you gain insight into this disorder, and if you are a mental health professional, I hope they will help deepen your knowledge of PTSD.

And, finally, I hope that my book will contribute to diminishing prejudices, discrimination, and stigmatization of those affected by PTSD.

I've often heard from military members with PTSD that they feel that only other participants in wars or peace missions can understand what they are going through. This is why I decided to write a book that focuses only on the experiences of service members and their families. I wanted them to feel connected when reading the stories and to know that others who have not walked in their shoes will be walking beside them as they read this book.

Leah Wizelman

An Introduction to Posttraumatic Stress Disorder

Imagine being awakened by the sound of claymores and machine gun and rifle fire in the pitch blackness that is suddenly lit up by flares and tracers. For a split second you don't know where the hell you are, then you fire your own rifle into the night. Then the weapons stop, and there is a new sound, but one heard before: Low moaning, somewhere out in the night. And it is black. Black until dawn.

But you aren't there anymore. You are in your bed at home, nearly 30 years later. And your bed and pillow are drenched with sweat.

～

The veteran who told this story is one of many suffering from posttraumatic stress disorder (PTSD). PTSD symptoms have been known for a very long time: They were described back in 4000 BC. In the eighth century BC, Homer wrote about them in his epic *Iliad* in connection with the battle for Troy. Several of the terms that were used for this disorder throughout centuries stood in relation to war trauma: "soldier's heart" during the American Civil War, "shell shock" during World War I, and "combat fatigue" during World War II. In 1980, it was included in the *Diagnostic and Statistical Manual of Mental Disorders* of the American Psychiatric Association as "posttraumatic stress disorder"; in 1992, it was introduced into the *International Classification of Diseases and Related Health Problems* of the World Health Organization.

Already during World War I or even sooner, military members with PTSD were discriminated against and labeled "cowards." Anyone exempted from combat because of this disorder was considered "dishonorable." Of course, suffering from PTSD has nothing to do with being a "wimp"—anyone going through a traumatic experience can develop PTSD.

A "trauma" involves actual or threatened death or serious injury and is of an extreme nature or catastrophic magnitude. The individual has either experienced or witnessed it or has learned that it happened to a family member or close friend. During the traumatic exposure, the person feels intense fear, helplessness, or horror. A trauma can be a one-time event with a sudden, acute threat to life (type I trauma), or it can be long lasting and repeated and consist of extreme traumatizations (type II trauma). Deployed service members may often be confronted with both types of trauma.

PTSD causes severe distress or impairment in relationships, at work, or in other areas of life. Its main symptoms are the following:

Reexperiencing of the traumatic event with all mental, emotional, and physical aspects, for example, as flashbacks, hallucinations, illusions, nightmares, or through recurrent and intrusive distressing recollections—When confronted with a trigger (see below), the functions of the brain area responsible for the differentiation between memory and presence are reduced. At the same time, the brain regions that contain memories of the traumatic event are being stimulated. This causes the person not to be able to distinguish, for a brief time, between the present time and the traumatic experience being relived as a flashback.

Avoidance of situations, activities, places, people, images, sounds, odors, taste sensations, feelings, or thoughts that remind the individual of the traumatic experience—The reason is that these so-called triggers can provoke enormous distress and physical responses like trembling, sweating, palpitations, breathing difficulties, nausea, gastrointestinal problems, or anxiety and panic attacks. The affected person may not remember part of or the whole trauma (= amnesia).

Emotional numbing, loss of emotions, particularly of loving and other positive feelings. The trauma survivor may feel detached, disconnected, or estranged from others, which may lead to withdrawal from society and loss of interest in former hobbies. The individual may also experience a sense of a foreshortened future and believe that his or her life span will be shorter than normal or that he or she will never have a family or career.

Hyperarousal of the vegetative nervous system, which shows itself in hypervigilance, an exaggerated startle response, difficulty falling or staying asleep, difficulty concentrating, irritability and outbursts of anger

People with PTSD may suffer from additional symptoms, like problems with self-esteem, self-blame, guilt, shame, despair, hopelessness, and others. The condition also has an influence on the body's biological systems, such as cardiovascular effects like an elevated heart rate, even during resting state or elevated blood pressure. It may also affect the nervous system, the hormonal systems, the anatomy and reactions of the brain, and the immune system.

Previous terms for PTSD, like "railway spine," "irritable heart," "soldier's heart," "disorderly action of the heart," and "neurocirculatory asthenia" already indicated physical symptoms appearing within the context of this disorder. The number of physical illness increases in people suffering from PTSD. For example, diseases of the gastrointestinal tract and the heart, neurological illnesses, arthritis, diabetes, psoriasis, headaches, chest pain, other pain symptoms, chronic fatigue syndrome, and other diseases often occur simultaneously with PTSD.

The development and course of PTSD may be highly variable between different individuals. Before developing actual PTSD, a trauma survivor may suffer from acute stress disorder (ASD), which occurs within a month after the traumatic event and lasts between two days and one month. ASD encompasses the same symptoms as PTSD and includes dissociative symptoms (see below) during or directly after the event.

However, not everyone who goes on to develop PTSD has experienced dissociation. If the symptoms do not subside after a month, one speaks of *acute PTSD* and, if they are still present after three months, of *chronic PTSD*. It can also happen that the symptoms emerge only after more than six months after the trauma (*delayed onset*). Even cases with extreme delays of almost fifty years have been reported.

The intensity of the individual symptoms can change for the better or worse over the course of time. They may be present decades after the event, but they may also vanish completely—or seem to do so and then, if triggered, recur in the future.

Dissociation during a traumatic experience is a protective mechanism that blends out particular perceptions of the event. As part of a mental disorder, dissociation can lead, for example, to serious amnesias, to a changed perception of the surroundings, to having the impression of seeing oneself from the outside, to feeling as if one is outside of one's body, or to disorientation regarding oneself.

However, mild forms of dissociation can also be experienced by healthy people, such as "driving automatically" without thinking or being transported by a touching movie.

People who have suffered very early or prolonged and extreme traumas may develop symptoms in addition to PTSD, such as problems with regulating impulses and emotions, dissociative symptoms, somatoform disorders (physical symptoms without organic cause), pathological changes in the perception of oneself, sexual disorders and dysfunctional relationships, self-harm/self-destructive action, and changes in fundamental convictions, religious beliefs, and moral concepts.

This clinical picture is called *Complex PTSD*, also known as *DESNOS* (disorders of extreme stress not otherwise specified).

A traumatic experience can have other psychological consequences besides PTSD. Thus, trauma survivors suffering from PTSD often have additional mental disorders, including major depression, bipolar disorder (formerly manic depression), generalized anxiety disorder, panic disorder, phobias (agoraphobia, social phobia, and specific phobias), alcohol and drug abuse, obsessive-compulsive disorder, dissociative disorders, personality disorders, and psychosomatic complaints (physical symptoms without organic cause).

About 5 to 50 percent of the people experiencing PTSD symptoms after a traumatic event go on to develop chronic PTSD. The statistics on the frequency of PTSD differ depending on the country, the sample, the method of diagnosis, and assessment. On the average, international studies found that about 5 percent suffer from PTSD at some point in their lives; in the United States, it is about 10 percent of females and 5 percent of males in the general adult population.

The National Vietnam Veterans Readjustment Survey estimated that almost 31 percent of all male and almost 27 percent of all female American Vietnam veterans suffered from PTSD at some point since returning from Vietnam. In addition, more than 22 percent of male and more than 21 percent of female Vietnam War veterans had a partial PTSD at some time.

A genetic predisposition, negative prebirth conditions, and traumatic experiences in early childhood increase the risk of developing PTSD after trauma. The same applies to concurrent and earlier negative experiences. In addition, a personal or a family history of mental disorders, like depression or anxiety disorders, can be a risk factor. The type, duration, and severity of the traumatic event and the proximity of an individual's exposure play a role in the development of PTSD (long-lasting, extreme traumas at the hands of other humans have the most severe effects), as do dissociative symptoms during or shortly after the trauma, repeated reexperiencing of the event, and the development of acute stress disorder.

An ASD does not have to lead to PTSD, however. Other vulnerability factors include personality traits (like low self-confidence), poor coping abilities, familial instability, lack of social support, and severe physical injuries and lasting disabilities.

On the other hand, particular genetic and neurobiological traits, positive familial experiences during early childhood, social support, and the absence of other risk factors contribute to a reduced vulnerability for PTSD. Good preparation for possibly traumatizing events of occupationally at-risk groups, like the military, police, firefighters, and emergency medical services, can also protect against PTSD.

Positive personal coping strategies, particularly taking concrete action to improve one's situation, self-confidence, optimism, and hope, as well as the attitude that one can influence one's life circumstances, can counteract the development of PTSD.

If you or a family member suffers from PTSD, there is help available: PTSD is now being treated by a variety of forms of psychotherapy, by medication, or by a combination of both. The length of the therapy depends on the complexity of the disorder and may vary strongly between different individuals. PTSD after a type I trauma can be treated within a short time period, while the therapy of PTSD after type II trauma and Complex PTSD can be far more complicated.

Stories from PTSD
Sufferers and Their Families

I Could Have Been
the Poster Child for PTSD

J.D.B. served in the U.S. Air Force for a total of twenty years, from 1966 through 1989. He spent ten years in the military police and ten years in aircrew training.

When I left Vietnam, I was not the same person who got off the plane a year earlier. I had a ticking time bomb in me and didn't know it. I knew I had changed, but I had no idea why. I tried as best as I could to function and act as normal as I could.

I had the PTSD "fuse," as I call it, planted in me during the Tet Offensive in 1968 when I experienced an event that made me feel terrified to the tenth power and in total panic.

However, my PTSD did not ignite till much later: the "bomb" went off in 1976 when my father suddenly died in February and my father-in-law three weeks later, also unexpectedly. That is all it took. Death up front and personal all over again.

I let it all out. My world came crashing in on me. I had mild to severe flashbacks, was totally obsessed with death and anxiety, fear, paranoia; I trusted no one, became a hermit and loner with no social life, avoided responsibility as much as possible, and jumped when the phone rang. I've been living in the "fight or flight" mode ever since.

I developed all the symptoms that encompass PTSD—I could have been the poster child for PTSD. However, I didn't seek help because in 1976 there was no such thing as PTSD. I was relieved of duty and admitted to a mental hospital for six weeks in 1979 for evaluation and treatment for an unrecognized ailment. They had no idea what they were looking at in me. This was two years before PTSD was even on the Department of Veterans Affairs' list of disabilities.

The air force said I could stay in as long as I kept my emotions under control. I was told to "suck it (whatever *it* is) in, or you're out, discharged" and that I would never carry a weapon again. I had to cross-train out of the military police to another field. I didn't want to throw away ten years' military service. I did "suck it in," but the family paid hell when I let it out on them.

I got so paranoid about death that I spent many nights in the USAF emergency room telling them I was going to die. I used to leave the house at 3 a.m. and just walk to get away from the house because it had "death" in it and felt just as if I were back in Vietnam, looking over a sandbag bunker, shooting at "death." If we traveled, I made notes of where all the hospitals were on the highway we were on. I just went to pieces. After thirty years of putting up with my PTSD, my wife left me. Any wonder?

Before January 31, 1968, I was as normal as normal gets—a wild young kid whose worst worry was finding a good drag race, something cold-necked to drink, and seeing something naked.

January 31 in 1968 changed that attitude. That was the first day of the rest of my life. I got a "Real World 101 wake-up call!"

I am on sixteen medications to help me cope. As a result of the traumatic experience, I am also suffering from depression, generalized anxiety disorder, and substance abuse disorder. I have a big problem with guilt. Why wasn't I there to help save two very close friends at the bunker? I let them down. I hope to be able to apologize to them in the hereafter.

I cry at the drop of a hat, just as if it were yesterday. It's a never-ending depression because of guilt.

I have a hard time expressing my feelings—I guess because I just don't want to talk about it. My older brother, my twin sister, and I once went to our uncle's home for a reunion in my sister's twelve-passenger van. As we were leaving again, I piled all the way in the back seat because I didn't want anyone behind me, out of habit. My uncle said, "Going to take a nap back there, huh?" My older brother spoke up before I could say anything: "No, he's just being his normal antisocial self."

I said under my breath, "Bite me!"

For the past almost thirty years I have been the black sheep. My brother and two sisters have "blackballed" me. They see me as a lazy bum. They think PTSD is pure bunk.

Dealing with other people almost tops the list of situations that are particularly difficult for me to deal with. Anything stressful triggers emotions I cannot control. You'd better never sneak up behind me and goose me even in jest. Someone is going to get hurt!

After my retirement from the air force, I had any number of jobs. I either quit before someone got hurt, or I was fired. Here again, my emotions got the best of me. The more stress I am under, the worse my symptoms get. I avoid stressful situations at all cost, which means I have resigned from society. I live by myself and cope one day at a time.

My PTSD came to the surface in 1976, but no one connected the dots till my Veterans Affairs evaluation in 2004. A psychiatrist at the VA said, after looking at all my medical records and an interview, that I have a definite case of PTSD. I have a medical folder showing all the counseling sessions I have had since 1976 that could fill the Library of Congress.

My disability was approved in two months. That was unheard of. Most VA disabilities take at least two years. I have been in and out of counseling for thirty-five years. I still experience 70 percent of the psychological and physical symptoms that I felt thirty-eight years ago.

I have noticed an improvement as long as I take my meds, and I tolerate flashbacks better than a few years ago. The rest of the symptoms of PTSD are alive and well, sorry to say. I can function only as long as I stay on my medications. I cannot allow myself to let go and go back to that hell. If I do, I can't control my emotions.

For the past year, every Wednesday I've been seeing a shrink and talk over whatever. He did tell me I need to "get a life." I had one once—a long time ago.

I was twenty years old at the time of the traumatic experience that was the original cause of my PTSD. Almost thirty-nine years have passed since then. My outlook on the future is pessimistic. I see no hope—not just for me but the world. I have grandchildren and two daughters who live in the area. I find comfort being with them.

Part of Him
Just Didn't Come Home

J.C.W.'s husband, a former U.S. Army National Guard, served in the military from 1996 to 2005, when he was medically discharged because of his back problems. He was in the artillery and the infantry and a vehicle mechanic. In 2003, he was deployed to Iraq as an infantryman.

In Iraq, my husband David got into an ambush where vans came up on both sides of the road. He and his men were being shot at as they tried to overtake the convoy. This experience was very traumatizing for him, as well as the searches he had to perform, going into the Iraqi households to look for weapons.

About two weeks after he came home, our dogs were barking one night. Before he went to Iraq, he would have just yelled at them to be quiet, but that night he jumped up. His boots and the flashlight were by the bed, and he grabbed them and went out the door. He came back a little later and said, "The perimeter is secure." I thought the wording, instead of saying, "Oh, there isn't anybody in the yard," was a little weird, but they had told us that there would be little odd things like that. So I really didn't think he had PTSD that night. I just noticed that something was different.

But he started doing a lot of those kinds of things and a lot of hole digging in the yard, so he would have a place to hide if he needed to. He also made a plastic and framework structure between our back door and the alley so that he could carry the trash out without anyone watching him. He was very jumpy. Every time a car drove by, he always looked to see who it was and if they stopped. He had trouble going to Wal-Mart because he couldn't check all the doors and see all the people at the same time, and he had a lot of trouble with being in public places. Before he went to Iraq, he wasn't that way.

By the time he was home two months, we were discussing that possibly he might have a problem and talked about how his head was not quite where it should be. We wondered if the intense back pain that he was having at this time was responsible for the odd things he would say or do. I think the first time we ever actually said PTSD was one day after he had been to the doctor. He said they tried to tell him at the doctor's office that the back pain was all in his head. My husband thought that the doctors were the ones that are crazy.

We live in a small town in rural Oklahoma. We're probably relatively safe from terrorism because we are a very unimportant little community as far as our world goes, but my husband would think that he saw someone watching us—he was convinced that someone was down the street, observing us. He wanted his whole family, children and grandchildren, right here all the time, for him to take care of.

He was having thoughts—I didn't know what they were—and he said he was having difficulties, he was having flashbacks and really bad dreams: he would have a dream where he was in Iraq and a lady was standing at the corner. But instead of holding an Iraqi baby, she would be holding one of our granddaughters. When that started happening, he really began to question if he was okay or not.

Eventually he put himself in the VA hospital, where they found out that he had a heart problem. They implanted a pacemaker, which helped somewhat but not a whole lot. At first he didn't want to go to the psychologist, to the groups, to the psychiatrist, because he was okay and he could fix himself.

It was probably two years before he actually admitted that maybe he needed some professional help for his mental problem also. At the VA hospital he was diagnosed with PTSD. He wanted no help whatsoever from us. He was going to take care of it. He thought he was doing a good job, and he didn't want to talk about it.

We had some really scary, really very rough times while he was trying to help himself. Just instantly he would get so angry as I've never seen him before. Later he admitted to me that that was when he couldn't tell the difference between being here in Oklahoma or being back in Iraq.

Now, when things start bothering him and he starts getting jumpy again, I can suggest that maybe he needs to start going to his groups a little more frequently, and he would think about it later and decide where he ought to go.

He still doesn't want help from the family. He will go to his group separately, he will talk online to some of the guys he went to Iraq with as well as with a lot of other people on the computer who also have been there, who also have PTSD. But as far as the family goes, he wants to keep all of that away from us and to protect us.

In the beginning, I tried to find everything I could on the Internet about PTSD, which is not a lot. There are many websites that have information, but it's all very sketchy. There is not actually any place that says, "This is how you cope with it."

So it's been trial and error. I would print stuff out and put it where I'd hope he would read it. I would send him e-mails with different sites I had visited. I don't know if he ever looked at any of them or not.

Now I help him more by just saying, "Honey, it seems like you're having a really rough day, do you need to talk about it?" which of course he always says no. But he tells me later that it's nice that I noticed that he's having a bad day.

He went through a six-week PTSD program: It seemed to help him a little bit with the coping skills and these—I call them episodes—don't happen as often, but when they do happen, they happen a lot worse.

Before my husband went to Iraq he was a very caring man; he would rather take care of you than let you know that there was anything wrong with him. He would do anything for a complete stranger if he thought they needed help. He is now very leery, very suspicious, and he sometimes is scary because he gets so angry so quickly, and he won't explain to you that he's having flashbacks.

Before, he was always a very touching person, and he doesn't want you to touch him now. He's like, "Let me exist over here, and you stay over there." He has horrible nightmares about people being in our house, holding our children hostage. He kicks and fights in his sleep a lot of times. He has flashbacks of when he had to tell his guys, "Today, this is what we are going to do."

But in the flashback it's not the men he was in charge of, it's our children. Our children are the age of those men. He has a lot of difficulties with keeping Iraq separate from now. He has a really hard time remembering anything, like how many inches are in a foot. He can't recall birthdays, or if it happened before September 11, he usually doesn't know what it was.

He can't remember things that are going on in town, like when the governor changes or so—anything outside of having to do with Iraq. Yet he can remember instantly a mass of details of everything he did while he was gone, but he can't remember things that happened right here at home since he's been back.

He used to do a lot of woodworking. He doesn't anymore, and I just thought he had no more interest in it, but I have recently found out it's because he can't remember the measurements and the angles and how you make things go together. That's really frustrating for him.

He lost interest in everything. He used to be a person who enjoyed going places—to the flea market, or an art festival, or an air show, or a fair. He hardly ever goes anyplace, unless he goes fishing or hunting by himself.

He's made our little property that we own safe, he's made it secure, and he prefers to stay home. He hates being in crowds. If we go someplace, he wants to sit with his back to a wall where he can watch the door. He is much more nervous now and has very little contact physically with any other people except our family.

My neighbors help me take care of him. They watch him, and when he starts doing things that they think are scary, they call me. He built an observation post in a tree in our yard. They called me and asked, "Do you know that he sits up there in that chair?" "Yes, I know he sits up in that chair." Or, "Do you know he's digging a new hole?"

He had a foxhole in our garden, and he had a foxhole in the front yard, and he had dug a great big foxhole under our house with enough supplies that he can put all of us under our house, and we can exist while whoever is doing whatever. I came home one day to find him in the foxhole in the garden, lying in the bottom of it, just crying and crying. When I touched him, he jumped like I was trying to kill him. He was not in our yard in his brain. I held him, and he cried and cried: he had just been working in the garden when he heard a noise and looked up, and he "saw" that people were in our yard—they had climbed the fence. That's the only time I've ever seen him actually completely disappear in a flashback.

My relatives try very hard just to treat him like they always have. They don't understand. They don't want to talk about it, and they don't want to learn anything about it. They just try to blow it off like nothing's going on. It's mostly "me and him against the world."

We have grown children. They still love Dad, but that he has PTSD scares them: he's Dad sometimes, and sometimes he's not Dad, and you never know which is going to be which. I sometimes say, "Yeah, I noticed he's a little bit weird right now." And then other times I'll say that he seems to be a whole lot more like Dad today.

There are just not enough things that you can explain to him to make him understand because *I* don't understand. There have been the few times that he's done things that really confused and upset the whole entire family and make us really wonder if we are doing what we should be, about taking care of him and such. He's apologized for it later, and we found information that helps us understand that we know nothing.

None of us are sorry he went to Iraq and did what he did. I was very proud that he went over there. But it's just that sometimes we get really sad because we ask ourselves, "Why did this have to happen to someone who is as good a man as he was?" He's just not himself—part of him just didn't come home. It's almost like there's a whole different person inside the body that we know as the husband or the Dad.

When he's having an episode, then sometimes we get out of the way, and sometimes we try to give him a helping hand; it depends on what's happening. Some of them have scared us to where we just hope that he doesn't do anything to hurt himself. I've never been scared that he's going to hurt us; it's more that I'm worried that he's going to get so tired of the episodes happening that his brain won't be able to rationalize and not harm himself. Normally I would never worry about him hurting himself, but when those episodes happen, I don't know. I don't know how much of the true him is still there to keep that from happening.

I think the biggest aspect and burden of PTSD for our family is the unpredictability. You don't know what's going to cause it to happen. A couple of times I have called a friend of his, and once his friend even came over and got his guns because David was being really different.

We don't know how to help him—should you leave him alone, should you try to talk to him, what do you do? You try to treat him the same, but you don't know if he's comprehending. When he has a bad dream, there's not a lot I can do, except to just let him know I am here, to let him know I am still his friend and I still love him.

PTSD is not like that you wake up and you realize you're having a bad day because of it or you're not. It happens in an instant. It can be something on TV, it can be some way I say a sentence, anything. . . . And sometimes nothing that we can figure out sets him off, so we're kind of like on alert all the time.

I don't know if it's gotten worse or better over the years, I think it runs in cycles: it seems like sometimes it's more prominent, and other times he's able to push it back a little more. I don't know what triggers those cycles. For example, we can watch a movie that has guns in it, and he'll be fine; we can watch the news, and he'll be fine; we can walk into a store, and there'll be a loud noise—and he won't be okay. But then next week we can walk into a store, and there'll be a loud noise, and it won't bother him.

Sometimes when we're in a store, he has to walk around and make sure that everybody there is safe and everybody is okay, and other times he will stay with me, and we'll just go through the store. There doesn't seem to be a whole lot of rhyme or reason in any of it.

My husband's PTSD has had a great traumatizing effect on me. I went back to the counselor, and I take a nerve pill now every day. I don't like feeling helpless, and I feel helpless because I should be able to fix him, I should be able to help him, and I can't.

I get up every day because I have no other choice, and I deal with what is thrown at me as it's thrown at me. I don't have a secret, I don't have a special formula, I can't say every time something happens, "This is what I do," because I don't know.

It depends on what's happening since there are always different situations. If he's sad and lets me touch him, I will touch him and reassure him. We assure each other that we still love each other regardless, and he knows that I'm not going to throw him away because he's different.

He knows that I'm standing behind him and that I will do whatever I can to help. In the bad times we just kind of muddle through, and in the good times we try to make up for the bad times. I always say that's probably the hardest part, that there's not a rhyme or reason, and there's no way for me to pick up the phone and call somebody that will fix him or find something on the Internet that will fix him.

So what helps me the most is the following: about four months ago, I decided I can't fix him. Instead of spending all my time and effort on that or on trying to find someone who can, I'm just going to have to accept and enjoy the good times and muddle my way through the bad ones. I'm lucky that I got as much of him back as I did. Some people didn't get that. So I guess it's just accepting the fact that this is what he has, and this is what we're dealing with, and somewhere down the road there'll be a reason for it. Maybe someday I can help somebody else cope. But I had to stop trying to find someone who can fix him.

A woman explained to me that while he was gone, something caused big enough trauma to him, to his life, or to his mentality that made the grown-up David hide because that's the only way he could cope with it. Someday he may be able to quit hiding, but maybe never.

Living with PTSD Has Become a Bearable Reality

The corporal was a member of the Canadian army from 1990 to 2001. He served primarily with the Royal Canadian Regiment as an infanteer.

Thirteen years ago, in 1994, I was with the Royal Canadian Regiment. I took part in the United Nations' Operation Harmony in the former Republic of Yugoslavia, in the Southern Sector around Zadar, which is now Croatia. I was twenty years old at that time. There I was engaged in what Canadians like to call peacekeeping operations, but there wasn't much peacekeeping going on; there was still fighting, and I was exposed to combat, trauma, and genocide. It was not a good place to be.

I was in operations during my whole six-month tour of duty. I was an infanteer, and that is kind of a pressure cooker. There were a couple of really bad incidents, and the majority of the time I was living in environments surrounded by threats or the high potential for threat from people or land mines and booby traps.

The first couple of times something bad happens, you're sort of in shock, and you're asking yourself, "Is this really happening, or is this some movie?" It's all around you—the sounds, the smells; it happens very fast, and you are very confused. It's not how you imagined it in your mind during training or movies. Once the horror of it all starts to sink in, you start to become terrified—you realize that you just survived something like that. Then your guts kick in, and you begin to react as a soldier. You just start doing your duty. As time goes on and the more these events happen, the fear does not become less, but you work your way through it quicker. Right after you go through such events, you have the feeling of extreme fatigue; you don't see the world the same anymore, and you've almost grown up years in a period of seconds. That's what I mostly remember; you are sort of like a zombie wandering around. But if you got another three, four, or five months to do, you don't really have much time to sit down and think about how this is affecting you; you just try to swallow it and carry on.

I had a couple of periods when I was overseas where I was really struggling with emotions: I became depressed and very angry and had difficulties controlling my feelings. But then I suppressed that, carried on with my job, and did what we had to do. It just starts to pull on your mind, so when your deployment is over, you have a lot on your plate.

Then, when you come home, you're sort of in a honeymoon period: you are so happy to be back with your family, friends, and the good life. You're a young man, you've saved up six months worth of salary, so you can do things you couldn't normally do, and you have a fairly good time. You don't really notice the PTSD symptoms right away. It's a slow process. They start very small, and they grow very slowly: you slowly stop sleeping, slowly start having problems controlling your emotions, and the flashbacks become more difficult to control. You start to get mood fluctuations, and your appetite goes out of whack. With me, all of a sudden it seemed like I had a limitless amount of energy: I started doing a lot of marathon running to try to run this out of me, but I just couldn't get rid of the anxiety. Then I started having breakdowns. At that point I was still in the military and in leadership positions. There was always the fear of people seeing what was going on behind that mask I was wearing. So, you live with that, and it compounds things till you start to self-medicate and drink in order to sleep because you don't know at the time that that's not helping you at all.

During my deployment, the battalion was my family—it was my soldier support, it was my connection. My ability to function in the civilian world started to really fall apart after I came home. The only place I seemed to be comfortable was back in my military battalion, where behavior qualities like being aggressive were encouraged. I slowly started finding excuses to withdraw from my family and friends on the outside because I became less and less confident with my emotional capabilities and my ability to express my thoughts and feelings. I basically ended up in a period where the military, my battalion, was everything to me. I became a very hard soldier, very professional, but a very hard man. Anything outside of that capacity didn't really exist. That went on for a period of years until that started to go too. There were some cracks that began to show up in my facade, and that terrified me—the thought that I could have a breakdown, or that I could be seen as weak, or that I could no longer carry out my functions which belonged to my responsibility.

So I put in for a remuster hearing, which basically means that you move to a different part of the military to pick up a trade. Let's say to go from being a combat soldier in the infantry to going to learn how to weld and fix trucks. I put in for that, figuring that I just had to get away from the hard life, and then maybe I would be able to balance out what was going on with me.

The problem was, when I withdrew myself from that battalion and went to a different part of the army, I ended up pulling away from the remaining soldier supports that I had. I sort of merged myself with young people, young recruits that were coming in, but I had absolutely no ability to communicate with them. And that was the first indication to me that I was way out of whack. My behavior, my mood fluctuations, and my ways of expressing myself were completely out of tune with what was coming off from civilian street. This basically destroyed a lot of what was left of my confidence and my ability to control myself.

At that point I completed my training like a good soldier, I taught my courses and all that, but it wasn't long after that that I had a couple of breakdowns. I started to cease to function, I didn't show up for work, and the military police came looking for me. I guess that was the first realization that what I have is serious and that I can't ignore it. There was some acknowledgment on my part that something was out of control and that I needed to fix it. I didn't know what it was and didn't understand what was going on with me, but I knew that I was hurting quite a bit.

My warrant officer marched me into a doctor's office; he forced me in, he didn't give me a choice. I could have said what I had to say and walked away and left it alone, but although I didn't like what the psychiatrist was telling me, I continued to go back and listened and then voluntarily went into recovery for it.

I was medically released from the military for PTSD in 2001. I still didn't do well for about two years after that. The following three years I've probably had the most significant gains. I've really come back to life so to speak: being able to engage with people a lot more, being able to feel productive, feeling your life is not passing you by.

I've been many years in recovery now, about six, seven years. For me the cognitive-behavioral therapy was a big help. Like most young men, I was just on autopilot; I didn't really have the maturity or the ability to reflect, to figure out what was going on inside of me. Everything was black and white, you had some rules you lived by, about getting to the next day when you're overseas. Cognitive-behavioral therapy allowed me to really understand what was going on. It helped me not to fear myself so much and to get to work through some of the confusion and the emotional instability. When the symptoms are really out of control, with the severe depression and anxiety disorders, you can't think, you can't concentrate, you can't focus, you can't contextualize what's going on around you and what people are saying to you. It's a horrible way to live. I learned again to think through a lot of things. This allowed me to make significant gains. It allowed me to live with PTSD—if I hadn't successfully figured out that portion of it, I think I would be still in a lot of trouble.

The drugs have been good and bad. Some of the side effects are not nice to live with. I have not done well under medications like Paxil and similar ones. You're just not yourself. When I was really not doing well, I was on a pretty heavy dose of an antipsychotic called Nozinan. I was also committed for a while to a psychiatric ward, where I was heavily medicated for two or three weeks. Now I am on Epival, which is a mood stabilizer and a miniseizure medication as well, since I also developed seizurelike symptoms during my flashbacks. They are like muscle cramps, and the vessels in my eyes burst. Epival seems to do the trick: I stopped having so many seizures during my flashbacks. I'm on Prozac for the depression, which works well, and I'm on sleeping meds. I'd like to not be on all this medication, but discontinuing it has never been successful: I tried to come off the sleep meds but went too many days without having proper sleep.

PTSD surely plays a very large role in what is going on with me: it still determines how well I sleep, while other times it determines how well I function during the next day, my schedule, my timings, how my moods are, how I interpret what people are saying to me, or how I'm feeling.

I still have the odd tremors during a flashback; I have problems with my guts sometimes because the anxiety has a negative affect on the gastrointestinal tract. I still have a lot of memory problems and sometimes concentration problems, especially if I am triggered.

I got a bit of agoraphobia when it comes to crowds. I can't stand being in situations where I don't have an exit and where I'm not in a position to control something; to a certain degree that depends on how I'm feeling. I do not respond well to aggressive personalities. I become triggered very easily with that—also, if I hear gunshots that I am not expecting or sudden loud noises. I still have a bit of a startle reaction if something scares me when I'm not prepared for it. There were times when I responded to trauma back here in Canada, whether it be a vehicle accident or something similar: once a little girl fell off a bike, and there was lots of blood. If I see something like that, it can knock me off my feet for a couple of days.

I do a lot of journaling, and I hope that today, I have a good understanding of many of my triggers and of what's going on inside of me, and so I'm able to reflect and work through a lot of the problems. I still am triggered, but I don't find the effects as severe. However, I can't look at any of the pictures from Croatia, any of the pictures of my friends there.

My anger escalates pretty quickly sometimes. I still consider it a problem, but I concentrate on it, and I am on medication. If someone were to start arguing with me, or push me, or shove me, then that could start a chain reaction. So I still live with that.

I have a lot of problems with intimacy, people touching me, people getting close to me. It's particularly hard on my wife. Some days, I'm just sort of very cold, very dead to people around me, but on other days, I can warm up and not let my PTSD affect me so much. I still withdraw; I need a period every day where I have to get away from everybody and just be left alone. If I don't get that, I become fatigued and agitated.

I think family and friends can help you especially with respect to your need to withdraw. The more they understand, the less personally they take your behavior. That's very important because if they don't understand your reactions and, like normal people, interpret your reactions as partly their responsibility, then that can do all the damage. If they understand that the emotions that are here and now have nothing to do with them but with fifteen years ago, that makes it a bit easier for them to understand the context of how you're reacting and what you're saying. I think that's the biggest, most important part. The more they have an understanding of the condition, the easier it is on everybody. Because if they don't, they don't have a realistic chance of staying in relation with that person since it's like being in a relationship with a blindfold. They are not seeing the reality as the veteran is seeing it: he is angry right now, but it's not because of anything his spouse said; it's because something she said made him remember—a memory that she can't see or doesn't want to see.

I try to use the analogy of being told I have diabetes: if I need help, I take my insulin and do what my doctors tell me, and then I should live a good life. As long as I stay in the routines, it should not be an issue. It's exactly the same with PTSD: I take my meds, I stay in the routines, and I avoid the things that cause and agitate the condition.

I'm still in counseling on a regular basis and take a lot of medication, but I've gotten to a place where I have regained a quality of life and of success at work. I have a fulfilling job; I am back in a different capacity in the soldiers' community helping them.

I work for the Department of Veterans Affairs in Canada for the federal government in a program designed to put peers back in relationships with people that served. The former service members working for the VA get some training to make sure they do their work safely, and then they are allowed to assist in the stages of recovery, providing social support and talking to those asking for help. For sure, most of the time, being around people that understand has a big impact on the person's life. It had a huge impact on me; it did a lot of good for me to be around other soldiers that had PTSD.

We're dealing with a lot of casualties right now in Afghanistan, and some of them are my friends who stayed in the army. It's very hard for me. I worry a bit that in the next time there'll be a lot of reminders, a lot of triggers that I will have to work my way through, so that will be tough. But I don't think that my life is going to be miserable.

When PTSD flares up again, it's a little frustrating because I can be feeling like I'm doing well, as I haven't had too many problems for some months, and then I have another spike of depression or anxiety. So I have to go back to the doctor and look at changing medication. We address the problem, and it seems to correct itself, and we move on.

My wife has a good understanding of PTSD. It's very frustrating for her sometimes, but she seems to be reasonably eager to learn about it when she needs to.

I'm pretty positive about life. There is still the reality of living with PTSD, but at the same time it's a bearable reality, and it's not something that you dwell on too much—you just accept it as a fact of life now.

PTSD really limits your long-term view, though: you always look just at the end of your nose—not ten, fifteen years down the road. You are always enjoying that cup of coffee or the sunrise. You are not really looking at what is ahead. You got to sort of force yourself to do that. I guess, for so many years you didn't think about the future, you only thought about surviving the day. That's what it is.

I Look at
Life Differently Now

Hauptfeldwebel (Sergeant Major) Frank served from 1990 to 2005. He worked in logistics in a battalion for electronic combat, at first in the army, then in the Joint Support Service of the German armed forces.

I was traumatized four years ago, during a suicide attack on our bus in Kabul, Afghanistan, right at the very end of our deployment. At that moment, I was not in pain; I only felt helpless and disoriented. I had no idea what was going on and had the feeling that we had driven off the road to the right and landed in a ditch, while we actually had been flung off a great bit to the left. It had come so unexpected, out of nowhere, as the saying goes: "One is dead before one realizes it." The first thing that came to my mind was our morning drink: it was the weekend of Pentecost, and I had arranged with a few of my friends at home to meet at our traditional Whit Monday market for a morning drink. "Well, our flight home today and our get-together probably won't work out," were my first thoughts. At that point I still had no idea what had happened. I also didn't even know by next morning that four of my comrades had died.

If I remember correctly, the first symptoms I developed afterwards were probably restlessness and insomnia—I only slept about twenty-five hours per week. I could hardly sleep during the night for fear, but I was not tired during the day. I was always running at full steam. That didn't worry me, however; it seemed normal to me at the time. So at first, I would not have said that I was changing or had changed.

I was in the military hospital for about two weeks. Afterwards, I had to drive to the base every day for five weeks for follow-up treatment, to have the wounds attended to, splinters removed, threads pulled and so on, then still every other and finally every third day. Thus, in the beginning, I didn't have any opportunity to be aware of my psychological problem since I was still kept busy with the physical one. I was in a wheelchair in the hospital, and afterwards I had to walk on crutches for many weeks. So for me, the most important thing was to get physically okay, to be able to walk normally again. I had no reason to worry about my psyche.

After about seven weeks, at a reintegration seminar for the contingent, the colonel approached me and suggested that I see a psychologist. My wife had been speaking with him, and I had been wondering who she was talking about, as it had seemed to me that she was speaking about someone I didn't know. I would have never guessed at that moment that the conversation was actually about me.

A few weeks later, I went to a military psychologist who referred me to the trauma specialists. Together with a comrade, I spent two weeks at a military hospital, and they diagnosed

PTSD. For a start, I now at least knew what was actually wrong with me. I was advised to undergo therapy and requested to do this closer to home in a civilian hospital since I didn't feel comfortable at the military hospital. About four months later, I was admitted to a hospital for nine weeks for trauma therapy. There was a swimming pool, a fitness room, hiking every Friday, and many other offers. I had lots of exercise and lost almost twenty-two pounds during these nine weeks. I felt really good there and actually thought that this would bring a great improvement, even if not a complete recovery, and that with that I would have overcome my illness.

Two days after my discharge from the hospital, I had to go to the base again. On my way there, I got stomach pains; I felt hot, broke out in sweat, and couldn't explain why. On the base it got even worse. A psychologist made another appointment for me with a trauma specialist at the military hospital. I went there with my comrade and was put on antidepressants within three weeks. I'm still taking them today. Not the same ones as then; I've tried several different ones and increased the doses. Some really attacked my stomach; others lost their effectiveness after a while. Half a year ago, we changed to a new medication, which is not supposed to make you addicted, but I cannot live without it anymore. During my first therapy as an inpatient, I took sleeping pills only—initially some to make me sleep through, then some to make me fall asleep, and then a combination of both. That worked more or less, but then my body got used to them, and they were no longer effective.

In the months that followed, I had two more unsuccessful attempts at trauma therapy.

After a lot of back-and-forth, I was declared unfit for duty by four medical departments—ENT, orthopedics, dermatology, and psychology. I was discharged in early 2006. In between, there was a lot of struggling, explaining, and excusing to questions like, "When are you coming back?" After the doctors had told me in September that I wouldn't be able to return to duty again, I had already asked myself how I should explain this to the others. That was a tough time since nobody had known about my PTSD yet.

Just recently, three German soldiers were killed. My wife told me in the morning that something again had happened in Afghanistan and that a few had died, and she tried to prepare me. I turned on the television, looked at the video text, and read about it on the computer. These are moments that take me back four years and make me relive everything in my mind. It was a terrible day. In the evening I drove to a friend, a former comrade who had been on the bus with me. Everything had been going through his mind again too. The bad thing is, you can try to push it back in your memory as far as you want, which I'm actually not doing since I know I have to live with it and that it is part of my life, but in situations like these, with news like this—I'm back in the bus again.

I often have panic attacks and flashbacks. It can be an odor that causes them, a crying child, or a cow bellowing in a way that almost sounds human. My problem is that while I was sitting in the bus and hearing the cries of my comrades of fear and pain, maybe even the death cries, I couldn't see anyone since I couldn't open my eyes. Now, if I'm shopping and a baby cries or two people are yelling at each other and I cannot see where it's coming from, then I'm sitting in the bus again, unable to do anything. In the beginning I often fled out of the store or went somewhere else. But running away doesn't change anything.

I'm almost constantly breaking out in sweat. I'm watching television in a T-shirt and shorts while my wife wraps herself up in a blanket. It almost seems as if I had my own built-in warm-water bottle—even though I'd rather feel cold than hot, for sweating is also a trigger for me: then it always feels as if warm blood were running down my face. My face had been badly damaged, and I remember the sensation well. Sweating, sitting in the sun or in the spotlight is terrible for me. Then I again feel how I'm being pulled out of the bus and leaned against a concrete post, and the sun was burning down already at eight in the morning, and I was unable to get away. It is still that way today. When I'm driving and I open the sunroof because the sun is shining, it feels good for a moment, but then I have to close it again to get away from the sun. When I'm mowing the lawn it's different since I'm moving or can sit down in the shade.

In over four years, I had about five nights during which I slept well. Otherwise, there has been no night without a dream. I've dreamt of being in Afghanistan several times yet never of the attack. I'm often in the past in my dreams but experience myself the way I am now. Sometimes I have to ponder whether this is reality or if it was a dream. I actually experience my dreams physically: sometimes I "feel" being shot at, feel the bullets entering my body. My wife tells me that I'm jerking in my sleep, tossing and turning, talking and lashing out. I've also often squeezed her arms so hard that she had blue blotches, but I cannot remember that. The dreams follow me for days and weeks, some dreams I'm dragging around for an eternity. I remember dreams from 2003 and 2004, which I still have vividly before me in my mind about four years later. They are so real that I have the feeling I'm playing a part in a movie.

I get easily startled now. This is also because I'm hard of hearing since the attack. If I'm not wearing both my hearing aids when I'm working outside and someone approaches me unnoticed from behind and touches me on my shoulder, I have to really watch out that I don't hurt the person. It's possible that this comes from the explosion in Afghanistan. This also came out of nowhere, and I was not prepared. I also get a big scare if a door slams behind me, for example. In addition, I have tinnitus since the trauma. I've also been suffering from anxiety disorders, especially during the nights when I think I have heard something.

I get irritated quickly. Many things upset me now; for example, when I'm driving and somebody makes a turn without giving a signal, I get very mad. Or when I go shopping and someone is using the parking space for the handicapped without a permit. My wife and my daughter try to keep me calm, for I often go up to the people or wait till they come out of the store and make a remark to them. Before, I would have held back, but now I address them directly. I don't know if this is right, but somehow I feel better afterwards.

Sometimes it's really very minor things that get me extremely upset. For example, if I want another glass of water and my daughter pulls the glass away from me. Or my wife and I are taking the dogs for a walk in the evening, and she is three or four steps ahead of me because I can't walk any faster since my legs are hurting. This gets me all worked up, which is nonsense of course, but it is that way.

I used to enjoy riding my Kawasaki motorcycle, which could make 300 kilometers per hour. The year after the attack I took it on the Autobahn, where I once had a Ferrari ahead of me. We were going 280 kilometers per hour., with me following behind at a distance of 1.50 meters. If he had slammed on his breaks, I would have smashed right into him. I didn't care about my life. The motorcycle was faster than I could think. At some point I told myself that it couldn't go on like this. I was afraid that I might do something irreversible. After that, I didn't ride my motorbike for a whole year, and the following year I sold it.

I often have the feeling that I have to take some kind of tablets. Rather than mixing myself a cocktail of antidepressants, sleeping pills, or whatever, I take magnesium or multivitamins because I have the impression that I'm doing better when I've taken a pill.

Depression has been another of my problems since the attack.

I'm also familiar with emotional numbing. Sometimes I could cry when watching *Lassie* on TV, and other times, I probably couldn't care less if somebody were to fall over dead in front of me. Often it feels as if I were empty inside, maybe like a rubber doll, an empty shell. One fades out feelings or doesn't allow them to surface. I also don't need to be hugged by my wife or feel that I need to hug her. I often feel like being dead.

My mood fluctuations have gotten a bit weaker due to the tablets. It still happens that I'm up one minute and down the next in an instant, but with the antidepressants I feel no euphoria and don't flip out to an extreme anymore. My mood is more on an even level now, and so I've become more predictable. Nevertheless, it may happen that when we intend to go to a celebration, I'll say in the last minute that I can't go. If I plan something in particular that I'd like to do, most of the time, it won't work out. I don't know if I'm afraid or what the reason is. If I have to go someplace, I feel as if I'm having a medicine ball in my stomach. It's all bloated, and I have problems with my digestion that day. I have the feeling that my body wants to fight against it, as if it would tell me, "You better stay home." Maybe it's because at home I feel the safest.

I liked playing soccer, volleyball, table tennis, and tennis—the only hobby I have now is my family, house, and garden. As far as friends go, as one so nicely says, "The social surroundings have broken down." But there's a lot more behind it. Many of our friends said at some time, "If you are always sick, can't do this or that, don't show up, don't feel like it, then there's no fun anymore." Often there are times when I just don't want to see anybody, when I just want to disappear, close the shutters, and be left in peace. Most friendships don't last under these conditions. When they said, "Well, just call when you feel like it," then that was usually it. The only one we are still friends with is my former comrade who sat in the bus with me.

The wife of our late neighbors used to say, "Frank is the only one who is always there when you need it. He always helps, instead of just standing there and watching." In the past it was indeed the case that whenever someone in the neighborhood was doing something, I asked if I could be of assistance. Today, I hide when I see a neighbor coming out of the house with a ladder. It's almost as if I were afraid that I might be asked for help.

My wife gives me lots of support. She looks after me, drives me on, and plans for me. If I were alone by myself, I probably wouldn't be alive now. I think, I wouldn't even wash myself once a day and would just lie in a corner. I'm really glad if I manage to wash myself before my daughter comes home from school around 2 p.m. My wife always says to me, "Go and get washed, then we can eat and do this or that in the afternoon." She urges me and also encourages me to work. If things would go according to me, nothing would get done; I have no drive anymore.

I never have the desire to talk about my experiences in Afghanistan with my wife. I'd rather talk to another patient in the hospital about my problems than to her, and this disappoints her. But I think the reason is that I don't want to burden her any more than I already do. She has enough problems with me as it is. So I try to manage by myself.

I often feel I should do something nice for everyone, like giving them presents. I can't say for certain why this is, but maybe so people like me and have a better opinion of me. I got to hear at the base, "He just doesn't feel like it, he's just a lazy bum and wants to get out of everything." Maybe I'm trying to make a good impression.

I used to be a cheerful person. I always said, "A day on duty, during which I didn't laugh, is a day lost," also in Afghanistan and Bosnia. I didn't want to go to bed at night without having laughed at least once. I said that if we didn't have anything to laugh about, we'd just have to make a reason. Today, in spite of everything, I probably still laugh once a day; I don't know, but I have become a lot more serious. I don't take many things as lightly as before, but on the other hand, I now have the feeling that I have to enjoy life more and to use it well. I used to worry, how I should pay off my house, pay for this or that, and now I say, why not buy a car on credit or take a vacation. Before, I would have said that we couldn't afford it; now I just do it or try to convince my wife. She says we have enough work at home, but I also have the need to get away from everything for a while and see nothing of the work here. I look at life differently now. If you have almost been at the end, you tell yourself that it may be over quickly and that you should enjoy each day you have.

If people ask me, how things are going, I say, "If it doesn't get any worse, it's okay." Of course, it's no high standard of living that I currently have. Someday I definitely would like to get to a point where I wake up in the morning at eight, after eight hours of sleep or at least seven or six, and not to get up at ten, eleven or twelve and then having merely slept for eight hours. Like every other normal person, I'd like to go to bed at night, sleep, wake up in the morning, and go to work. I'd like to still have a purpose and responsibility. I'll be thirty-eight next week; should I sit at home and wait till I die? At the moment, I'm doing volunteer work for a social organization a few hours a week. I also would like to earn a little bit of money. But at the moment, I wouldn't know what job to do, and I also wouldn't have the necessary drive. I'm glad if I even get the cleaning of my car done or some painting in the garage. Something inside myself is blocking me. Sometimes I don't know how I used to manage before: I left the house in the morning at a quarter to seven, went to the base, came home ten to twelve hours later, mowed the lawn, did this and that. I hope someday to get back to that old life again and that my wife can send me somewhere or ask me to do something and not having to feel that without her I'm stuck. But that's indeed the truth: without her, many of my days would probably be spent lying on the couch.

PTSD is not known enough yet. Officially, we are not at war in Afghanistan, but where is the difference? More and more will be suffering from PTSD. I'm just hoping that the people who are not affected will show understanding. I don't mean pity but understanding of the situation. I was thirty-four when it happened, and everyone said, "You don't have to quit the service; what do you want to do then?" I was retired at thirty-six; it was not my choice. Who asked my four comrades, who were between twenty-four and thirty-one, if they wanted to die? Or the comrade who lost an eye and a leg at twenty-one? Nobody asked him either if he wanted to come back an invalid.

What also makes it bad afterwards is the battle for recognition and compensation.

Two, three years ago, at the birthday party of my wife, a neighbor said to my friend, who also had lost an eye in the attack, "It's the fault of your wives that you don't go back to your unit. They should kick you in the ass because it's your goddamn duty to go there." What a nice birthday that turned out to be! This lack of understanding is terrible and also when somebody says, we had an accident—it was no accident, someone tried to kill me. There's a difference if I slide into the ditch with my car or some camel driver tries to blow me up with 150 kilos of dynamite.

Maybe it was an additional burden that we were already on our way home, that we had done our duty and had concluded our deployment. We were thinking of home. I had two bottles of bubble wine and seven cans of beer with me; I could have defended myself with these. We were in a holiday mood, not a combat mood.

If someone doesn't know PTSD, he cannot imagine it.

If I were living alone by myself, I wouldn't care anymore and say, "Things are good enough for me the way they are." But my wife is thirty-eight, my daughter almost fifteen, we are not old people. We'd like to still get something out of life, not have to say one day that everything was shit. We'd like to be able to look ahead, but at the moment, I wouldn't know where to look.

A Part of
Me Died That Night

Ex-Staff Sergeant Michael joined the Texas Army National Guard in 1997 and was on active duty from 1998 to 2006 in the U.S. Army field artillery. He served two tours in Iraq, in 2003 and 2005. He was twenty-six years old during his first deployment, when he was part of an event that he considers the main cause of his PTSD: He and other U.S. soldiers had just shot three men who were attempting to run a checkpoint. Then a family of six was trying to cross the checkpoint in their car and, by a terrible mistake, ended up being shot by them too. Only the mother and one of the children survived. Michael believes that his bullets hit eight-year-old Mirvet, who died despite his and others' attempts to save her life.

It has been three years since the night Mirvet was killed by the hands of U.S. soldiers and myself in Baghdad, Iraq, in 2003. I remember it being quiet and almost tranquil; I felt like it was happening but at the same time like it wasn't happening. I felt scared but safe, and I felt like breaking down and crying. I was as if in a trance, and whenever I think and remember that night, I see it all from above with myself on the ground along with the event.

A part of me died with that little girl that night.

I started experiencing PTSD symptoms after many traumatic events during my two tours in Iraq: multiple kills, gunfights, IED attacks, the handling of numerous dead bodies—both American and enemy—and the killing of Mirvet. The nightmares started up first, then, as the experiences got worse and more current, the chest pains, shakes, sweating, and anxiety and panic attacks got severe.

After I came home from my first tour in Iraq, I used binge drinking to ease my anxiety. The memories of these gruesome experiences went away after several months but started bothering me again when I deployed to Iraq a second time in late 2005. The people and odors there triggered these intrusive thoughts. I was diagnosed with PTSD by two mental health professionals in a combat support hospital in Iraq. My unit decided it was time to relieve me of my position, which was NCOIC of Taji Main Entry. I had provided a group of Iraqi kids with construction materials that I had found in a trash bin and got an other-than-honorable discharge. My attraction and loyalty to the Iraqi kids came from feeling regret for the death of Mirvet, and this is why I devoted all my attention to them.

After a lot of research on PTSD, I realized that it was these symptoms that led to excessive drinking, distancing myself from my family and kids, depression, and sleepless nights. I sought help on my own. After my discharge I was jobless and tried to work in a telemarketing center, but that gave me too much time to think about my war-related issues. I tend to think a lot of Iraq and the events that happened there.

I always feel disconnected from the world around me and the things that happen to me and sometimes more than I care for. I feel physically numb, like I'm falling. It's hard to play with my own daughters, I no longer feel like being active, I feel a lot of guilt and depression. I wish I could take back what I did. Distancing myself from my kids probably makes me feel the worst. I killed an eight-year-old kid in Iraq, and to me it's not fair that my children get to live on here in the U.S. while that lady in Iraq will never see her daughter again.

Sometimes I feel like I need to stand my guard a 100 percent. This gets in the way of my marriage and relationships with my kids.

I feel bad for all the lives I took and handled in Iraq, U.S. troops, Mirvet . . . , although I didn't know them. I touched their lifeless bodies, and I feel connected to their families now and somewhat responsible. I don't know why, but I do.

PTSD is slowly killing me inside. I suffer from manic depression and alcohol dependency. I feel claustrophobic in enclosed areas and lost at times. I noticed that I'm prone to a lot of anger, and I overreact a lot more now. I'm always arguing with my wife, I feel disrespected easily, and I tie it all to the events. I get really touchy when I hear someone say that we don't belong in Iraq or that we get what we deserve for being there. I once choked a man for saying those things to me.

For some reason I am still afraid of dying out there, although I know it couldn't happen. Thus, I make excuses to stay in the house, and I make it a point to tell my employer to work me to death. I am currently looking for a second job to help me cope with this. I work to keep my mind off the thoughts of Iraq, but it's a never-ending cycle because something or someone will trigger my thoughts.

My flashbacks are provoked by certain smells, colors, noises, music, and speech. In particular I remember the time I was watching the documentary *The War Tapes* and seeing a scene in the movie where a car bomb exploded at a main gate of Camp Taji. The sound of the car bomb going off triggered a flashback of the distinctive sound of the power transformer shutting off in the quiet Baghdad night, the night that I helped kill Mirvet. When I research the Internet and find videos on IED attacks, they trigger my feelings and thoughts of an IED incident.

One time while we were driving from Dallas to Killeen after a weekend visit to my in-laws, I yelled at my wife when I woke up from a nightmare, to "watch out for the rail and watch out for the IED," scaring her and making her swerve to the other lane of the highway.

I go through at least three anxiety attacks a week due to flashbacks, nightmares, and stress. The symptoms include a pounding heart, troubled breathing, tightness of the chest, feeling shaky and sweaty. I also experience headaches and dizziness. The physical symptoms usually occur when I think about the incidents and the body parts and blood. My anxiety is provoked by thoughts of my buddies dying; I get emotional real easy when I see family reunions after the return of the troops from Iraq because deep down I know that someone will not come back to their family. Death scenes showing reality are really hard to take, and those scenes make my chest tighten. At the same time however, I am obsessed with the insurgency and constantly need to watch Iraq-related news.

I suffer from insomnia and nightmares. I've had a recurrent nightmare during which I am being chased in Iraq and then hide in a house. I see cars driving to the house to bomb it, but then I realize that it is my family that is in the house, not me. At that point I wake up.

I am currently working as a bail bondsman, doing fifteen-hour nights from Sunday to Wednesday just to avoid sleeping at night. I prefer to sleep during the day because I have more of a chance of getting bothered during the days than during the nights.

All I do nowadays is work and drink. I feel really uncomfortable around strangers and tend to be a little overprotective. This was especially the case with my family when they still were part of my everyday life.

It was helpful to me when I found out that PTSD is a real disorder, but it needs to be addressed a little better than it is now. I'm still undergoing therapy—one-on-one counseling at the Vet Center—but I don't feel any improvement yet. I take no medication.

The best assistance others can give me is being supportive and listening, although at times I felt it was worthless talking to my wife about anything that happened in Iraq. I keep in touch only with the soldiers that have been out there with me, and my marriage has been deteriorating slowly. I'm going through a divorce right now, after seven years of marriage and four children. I feel useless like the Vietnam vets felt when they got back. I cannot provide for my family like I used to, I feel no desire to be with my kids, I feel lost and as if I don't have control of my life.

Dealing with the deaths of my fellow brothers and watching children and innocent people die will be forever in my mind.

I Believed I Did Not Have a Problem

Peter is a former Royal Australian Air Force (RAAF) Reserve staff sergeant and army corporal who served between 1960 and 1969. He spent four years in the Australian Cadets Air Training Corps, three years in the RAAF Reserve, and two years in the national service in the army, where he was a section commander in the infantry.

I was twenty-two years of age when I experienced the death of a close mate in military action during the Vietnam conflict thirty-nine years ago. Time slowed down to slow motion, and sound seemed to dissipate with a sensation of emptiness. The sight was clear, as everything around was quite vivid, but the feeling of detachment and isolation was strong.

After the event I served out my overseas service period in Vietnam. I developed a feeling of loneliness and started withdrawing from other people. I believe I had the symptoms of

PTSD very early after the incident but managed to control and hide the problem, generally believing that I really did not have a problem. I left the military about thirty years ago. I finally admitted to myself that I am suffering from a serious problem when I was becoming excessively stressed at my work and realized that I was not keeping my problems under control as well as I would have liked to. This built up over some years but reached a peak approximately six years ago. I decided to seek help and was diagnosed with PTSD about forty years after the traumatic event. I saw a psychiatrist at that time, which was of some help. As I did not open up fully to him because of my reluctance to trust him completely, I believe the improvement process took a lot longer than normal, though. Several years ago a counselor helped by making me realize that some of the things I was blaming myself for were not my fault.

PTSD has made me become more of a loner. I don't confide in anyone and maintain a barrier to keep people out. I don't allow anyone to see inside me and have always kept my problems to myself. I often feel a desire to be alone, for then one does not have to explain or answer the queries that come from people in one's presence; one does not wish to search and explain the depths of one's thoughts, which are trying to escape. One feels emotionally very vulnerable and helpless; when being alone it is easier to keep one's problems under wraps or out of the eyes of others. At times of sadness I don't want to be a burden to others nor explain myself. The help offered is not wanted, as it has not worked previously and is irritating. When I am sad I now know it will pass, and I don't want to have to make an effort to put on a front for others. During the sad moments it is hard to push away melancholic thoughts of the past, and I assume it would be a pain for other people to have to put up with it.

I have been more comfortable on a one-to-one basis. Dealing with groups of people became very difficult for me and causes me great anxiety. The physical symptoms are obvious. On most occasions they cannot be hidden from the observers, which creates greater and further anxiety. Situations where I am under the observation of numerous people make me uncomfortable and nervous—the only cure or prevention seems to be to ensure I don't place myself in such situations. This is nearly impossible on all occasions. Attending funerals or ceremonies are such uneasy events.

Some nights I have affected sleep. During such sleepless nights, unpleasant memories of past incidents are very vivid in my mind and keep coming back when I try to push them away. Time, especially in the early hours of the morning, drags on very slowly.

I'm suffering from paranoia, particularly concerning the safety of people I care about and tend to be overprotective. If a loved one is delayed or unreachable, I get overreactive. I would move mountains to ensure their well-being. I am on edge, ready to act, imaging the worst has happened. If, for example, they are out late at night or traveling alone, I sense their vulnerability. I have the possible danger magnified in my mind. I can't relax until I become aware that the situation is safe, and then I slowly calm down.

Seeing war-related news on TV is difficult for me too. I am also suffering from some anxiety as a result of the traumatic event, and I am aware I could be drinking less than I do. Over a period of time I had a better control of drinking.

None of the PTSD symptoms disappeared altogether—they have reduced but return on occasion with less intensity. Only the time spent in the country, away from the population, is not influenced by my PTSD. I have retired from the work force, which has reduced the work pressures. This has helped a great deal, as I am more relaxed in my everyday activities. My hope for my future is to have a reasonably comfortable existence.

He Thought I Was Telling Him He Was Crazy

Cathy is married to a Vietnam veteran who served as a U.S. Army Ranger, specializing in long-range reconnaissance patrol, from 1967 to 1971. He won the Bronze Star for heroism, but he won't tell her what he did to get it.

It wasn't one, but many traumatizing events, that caused my husband's PTSD:

He told me about sitting in a foxhole with his captain. As his captain was reading a letter from home, he was shot right through the letter into his heart and killed instantly. It was so fast the captain was still holding the letter in the sitting position when my husband discovered that he was dead.

Another time, my husband came upon a village that had just had chemicals sprayed over it that had killed every living creature. He said they looked as if their skin and fur was carefully taken off of them, and they had dropped where they stood.

He also participated in a raid on a POW camp. When they executed it, however, the prisoners had already been relocated. His squad was ambushed a few times as well.

I met my husband in 1990. His first wife had left him. I noticed very soon into our relationship that there would be certain changes in his mood and that particular things would set him off. He had a hair-trigger temper and reaction to sudden noises or other stimuli. If there was a large gathering of people and there was a lot of noise, he would become very agitated to the point where he'd be yelling at me or someone else at the top of his voice and get into physical confrontations very easily. He also had no eye for the future: he would use up the money or the food, not budgeting it out to make it last for a specific period of time.

I had seen a report on TV a few years ago about a program that treated PTSD in combat veterans and that the federal government was getting ready to close. The symptoms that were highlighted seemed to fit my husband to a tee. I recalled this program after we had been together for about three months and told him about it. I also said that I believed he had all the symptoms and that he could get treatment for it at the VA.

My husband thought I was telling him he was crazy. I explained that if there is treatment that will make you feel better and you don't get it, *that* is crazy. He fought me tooth and nail. I eventually got him to see a psychiatrist by having him go through the ratings process for his VA compensation. Money can be a great motivator. It was decided his PTSD was severe enough that he should go to the National Center for PTSD—after much prodding on my part. Getting him to actually go was another battle all by itself—it took me two years.

After treatment he was released and sent back to Los Angeles, where they assigned him a student psychologist that had absolutely no idea what it was to be a combat veteran. My husband left, never to return.

He had not accepted psychological help from anyone for the next twelve years. I was always trying to get him help other than pills issued to him by the VA and tried to reason with him but had no success. He and I got into a physical altercation, and it was through the courts that I was able to secure him the help he needs.

Now I try to help him by approaching him with calm determination.

When my husband and I first met, we were homeless, and he would deck anyone that approached either of us with a less than friendly tone, and that included his friends too—not many of them around anymore.

We have had a home for about nine years now. My husband has a very hard time sleeping at night, and I honestly don't know how he manages to keep the frustration he experiences every night from getting the best of him. He is actually more comfortable sleeping when he is outside than inside: when we were homeless, he had little trouble falling and staying asleep throughout the night. He says he feels safer when he's not "boxed in," and he used to be able to feel safe enough to sleep at night. But now that we are living inside, he will stay up most of the night and get some sleep during the day. He also sleeps better when there is noise around him.

My husband has attacked people that were just walking by, believing they were the "enemy." If we were walking or sitting outside somewhere and someone stopped to look at the scenery or the buildings, he would freak out and swear they were going to attack us. "They" were anyone that he didn't recognize as part of the citizenry of the town. Now this posed a real problem, as it was a tourist town! If there was a helicopter overhead at the same time, he really freaked out. He would run over to the people and start yelling and screaming at them and the helicopter that they weren't going to hurt us, *they* were going to get hurt if they didn't leave *now*! I would try to let him know that people weren't paying attention to us—in point of fact, they probably couldn't care less about us—but to no avail.

His response to uncomfortable situations was to become enraged and lash out both verbally and physically. Once my husband almost killed a guy just because he startled him: the man had walked up behind him, yelled out his name, and pushed him gently in the back. My husband turned around and let go with a roundhouse kick that hit the man in the chest, and after he fell, my husband pounced on him and attempted to take the guy's eyeball out. All this happened in about three seconds. I was across the street and sprinted over to him to try and pull him off the man before he did any more harm. I did not know it at the time, but my husband had already hit the man in the throat as he was falling. You see, my husband was a Ranger, and his MOS was long-range recon patrol with the 101st. He was trained to respond instantly and effectively during his missions. He was never untrained not to respond in this manner when he returned home.

There were other incidents as well, like when we first went to the VA to begin the doctor visits to get his claim processed. He was so nervous and anxious when they wouldn't tell him the results of the tests he had taken, he threw papers and books all over the office, overturned a desk, and called everyone in there everything but a child of God. Needless to say, he was immediately escorted out—without test results.

He says, looking back on things after his release from the military, the problems with his first marriage were mostly due to his undiagnosed PTSD. He tells me he was having nightmares from the time he returned in 1971. He had worked on a ranch till 1981 but had trouble holding employment afterwards. He thinks it was due to deep depression as well as him self-medicating with heroin.

Friends and family reacted to my husband's diagnosis by telling him, "There is nothing wrong with you, you just have a bad temper!"

My husband has very few contacts with anyone anymore. He is very dependent on me for human interaction.

The isolation and the grief of handling him, so he won't get into more legal trouble, is the greatest burden of PTSD for me. His disorder has had a traumatizing effect on me too. I am now much more reticent to argue or go out by myself as "*they* are going to get me, or I am going to leave him." His insecurities are such that he didn't believe I would stay and not abandon him for someone else. This is not as much of a problem as it was but is still there.

I really don't socialize, as I am worried about him flipping out on someone. His actions and reactions are so unpredictable that I just don't put anyone in that position, including myself. His flight-or-fight response is always just a hair's breadth away, and it takes him at least one whole day to stand down.

I have a support group that helps me stay sane, and that is my saving grace.

My husband is not a "terrorizing monster." The PTSD he has been trying to deal with is. People that have this disorder, including him, have a terrible time trusting anyone, including himself. The VA chief psychiatrist told me he had not seen a more profound case in the twenty-two years he had been practicing. I was also informed that I could probably expect my husband to either commit suicide or suicide by cop within ten years. His determination not to let this disorder get the better of him makes me very proud.

When I met my husband, he was very paranoid, combative, and could twist a thought or action that was meant for good into an evil ugly event. Now he is much more willing to see that not all situations are dangerous and deadly or that even most are not.

He is doing better these days, but as with everything else in life, some days are better than others. He has gotten clean and sober, which was a problem for the better part of our marriage. He has gone through court-ordered counseling and has come to see his disorder as a normal part of trauma. He has thus far refused psychological therapy, but nowadays we try to sit and reason things out so they don't appear so threatening anymore. He is much easier to talk and reason with than before, although, as with anyone else, this varies from day to day.

I'll Never Be
What I Was Before

Chief Petty Officer Second Class CD2 Retd. P. served in the Canadian navy from 1968 to 2004, which included twenty-five years' sea time. He was boatswain's mate, chief boatswain's mate, coxswain, deck officer, demolitions and small-arms instructor as well as senior instructor, and standards CPO and in other positions in the Seamanship Division. He participated in three NATO deployments and numerous antisubmarine patrols and was a UN observer in Cambodia in 1993.

It was in 1993, when I was forty-two: I was part of the UN forces and employed as an observer at that time. There was a murder involving a young woman in Cambodia, which was quite messy. I also saw children killed. That pretty much caused all my problems. I felt angry and ashamed because there wasn't anything I could do—I couldn't stop it. This was very upsetting. I felt guilt more than anything else.

It was quite a long time before I sought help; I was diagnosed with PTSD in 2000:

I was on the ship and in a mess with nine other people. They were always complaining that I was keeping them awake. I thought it was from snoring because nobody told me what it was all about. I guess they complained to the doctor on board, and the doctor sent me up to the hospital. I figured I was going there for a sleep apnea test or something like that, and I ended up in a psyche ward, doing all manner of testing and interviews. That's when I was diagnosed. Until then I hadn't realized that I had a problem. Well, I suppose I did, but I have always been fairly physical in a way. If you're taking the military for your life, then you express yourself a lot differently than you do with civilians. I was never in trouble, but I ended up in a lot of physical confrontations with mess mates and caused a lot of embarrassing incidents, so that's basically how I came to understand that I had a problem.

At the time of my diagnosis I was the chief boatswain's mate on the *Vancouver*, which is one of our destroyers. I had no outside interests at all, so I pretty much involved myself: I looked for work to do, I lived for the job, because that's what I knew and did since I was seventeen years old. I would spend the bulk of my time on the ship, and even when I could go home, I wouldn't. For me, the most important thing was to keep busy. Since I have never been a civilian, I was terrified of getting out of the service, especially at that time. So I stayed with what I knew.

When I first came back from Cambodia, I didn't like to go out in public at all and mostly stayed in my home. I was easily angered and very short tempered; I wouldn't take the time to argue with anybody—I'd fight them. Once I was diagnosed and put on medication, this behavior pretty much went away.

I couldn't remember things—I'd be in a conversation, and I would lose track of what was happening. I started out for work one day and ended up in another place where I hadn't intended to go, and I had no idea how I got there. Or I've gone to the store to get something specific and then couldn't remember for the life of me what it was. My memory still isn't as good as it used to be anymore. If I look at a phone number to call someone, I have to look at it five or six times to make sure I've got all the numbers right.

I feel tense and am easily nervous. Due to the medication, I am pretty mellow now. But I used to have anxiety or panic attacks that were quite severe. Certain smells and sounds, for example, trigger a response like that. Sometimes I feel closed in and trapped—when I feel an anxiety attack coming on and I can't stop it. I can't get away from it because I just don't know how to get out of it.

I experience flashbacks, which are mostly image driven. If I'm in China Town, sometimes just seeing an Asian makes me get a flashback, especially in the marketplaces because every village I was in had marketplaces. Once I realize what it is, I can calm down. I don't even know how to describe a flashback, but it's over fairly quickly once you realize where you are and that you are safe.

I don't try to avoid situations that could remind me of my traumatic experiences. That would pretty much be futile because I can't control what would do it. So I just try and put up with it as best as I can. And of course medication makes it a lot easier.

News bother me, especially when they show flashes of villages that have been burnt or children and people having been burnt, body parts, that kind of thing upsets me. And if it catches me off guard: my son was watching the movie *Fahrenheit 911*, and I wasn't paying any attention to what he was doing. When I walked by, there was an older woman in the movie, holding up a burnt baby, and I lost track of about two hours. I don't know what the hell happened. I figure it's things that you can't anticipate or avoid. If I have any kind of idea they're coming or if I'm prepared for something, then I usually can handle it. War-related movies on TV don't bother me because they are not the real thing—I've lived through the real thing. My wife can't understand why I still like to watch military and read military history. I think it's mostly because that's what I've done all my life. I like to feel associated with it; I'm retired now, but the job I do keeps me in contact with military people, and I understand the culture. So I never really had to become a civilian, at least not yet.

I sleep maybe two hours at a time and am usually up at five in the morning, but I think a lot of that has to do with trying to avoid sleep so I won't have the nightmares. I've had them fairly often ever since 1994. This has its effect on my health as well.

I have psoriasis, and the stress really brings it on. It got an awful lot worse after I came back from Cambodia. I have chronic pain, but it's from various things in my military career. Most of my time in the service was spent on ships, so I pretty much wore everything out. I would attribute some of the pain to the operational stress injury, but I don't know, that's just my own opinion.

I went through a divorce within six months of coming back. I also had trouble staying close with my children. When my father died, I felt nothing, although I had been very close to him. It was almost like I was the only one who didn't care. I deeply regret him dying, but it didn't cause me any discomfort. I recently remarried, and if my wife were to decide that she was leaving tomorrow, I don't think it would upset me. Of course, I would be sad, but I wouldn't freak out over that type of thing.

I used to be a fairly outgoing person, but now I don't go anywhere at all. If my wife wants to go somewhere on the weekends, I'll drive her, and if we're in a store and I get nervous, she understands. So I'll go and sit in the car.

I was an adept woodworker, but I don't do anything like that anymore—I just don't feel any motivation to do it. My wife said her sister wanted a table, and she volunteered me to make it, so I did. But it wasn't something that I would have started; it was something that I felt obliged to do, and I didn't get any joy out of it.

I also don't have the energy I used to have at all. So, I pretty much work and go home. I find that if I'm really upset, I'll go and play a video game for twenty minutes or so until I get past it. The game sort of absorbs me so I don't have time to think about other stuff.

I have been seeing a psychiatrist on a regular basis since 2000. Just doing that pretty much keeps me grounded. I started taking Welbutrin after my diagnosis, which worked quite well. They increased the dosage, and I felt pretty good, but I was still having a lot of anxiety attacks, so they put me on Effexor as well. That seems to have cut down the amount of anxiety attacks I've had. I don't know whether it's because that's what I expect the pill to do or whether that's what the pill is really doing. I also don't get angry as much. I'm fairly hard to get emotional about anything, and yet again, I could be sitting watching the TV, and tears will build up, and I have no idea why. It doesn't really matter what I'm watching, it's just something in it, something that's happened during the day maybe—I don't know, for unexplained reasons I'll just start tearing up.

I also have depression, but I take medication for it, so I sort of feel like, "just wait until it's over." Spend one day at a time, and then when your time is up, your time is up. It's kind of a strange philosophy, but that's how I feel life is.

As for my therapy, I just basically go and visit my therapist. She'll ask me how my week went, and I'll tell her. She knows I work with military people with PTSD. If I have difficulties, she is the first person I call—she has helped me a great deal. That's why I approach my therapist rather than try and go it alone. I also call her when I'm faced with a case I can't deal with. Sometimes working with people with PTSD is overwhelming, and sometimes my work is just flat boring, if there's nothing going on. But now we're involved in Afghanistan, and we are suffering more combat-related deaths—in contrast to our deployment in Cambodia when we were mostly confronted with hostilities, crimes, and corruption but not directly engaged in combat. The problem I see there is that most of the guys that I deal with were peacekeepers: we were put in countries that were at peace at that time, and most of us weren't armed. We usually worked in two-men teams or on our own and had no support from anybody, so we pretty much had to fend for ourselves. The training that we got before we went in was minimal because we had to deploy in a hurry. The rotation I was in in Cambodia required seamen for river patrols and boarding operations and confiscating illegal weapons. I spent my whole career as a boatswain, a trade that controls small boats and trains people to operate them. We patrolled well over 600 kilometers of rivers within Cambodia, which was very dangerous. You're out in the open, and the Khmer Rouge could be anywhere around, and that's who we were looking for. They were quick to fire at you. The locals were mostly involved in smuggling, so if you came across them stealing pigs or smuggling dope, they'd open up on you. You never knew who was going to shoot at you, and you could count on them being drunk in the afternoon and that they would shoot at anything that struck them as funny. There is nothing more dangerous than a twelve-year-old boy armed with an AK 47. I was there for seven months and can't begin to explain my experiences. The point being is, our soldiers who are in Afghanistan now are with their units, and they are with friends, and they are trained in combat, and they are doing what they know. So when they come back, most of them are going to be the "cock of the walk." They will be the most experienced combat troops we've had since the Korean conflict, and all the people I work with are feeling even more guilty about their efforts in peacekeeping areas. They want to go over there to Afghanistan and try to make up for the mistakes that they think they made, and that just can't happen. But that's how they feel, and they are going to feel much worse when these guys are walking around the bases with all their medals and everything else. We figure, we should have been able to handle it, but it didn't happen like that.

As for my PTSD, it is almost like an old friend now. I've had all the symptoms that I managed to live with for the last twelve years and everything else that goes with it. I think I'd actually miss them if I didn't have them anymore. I think I've learned to live with them. They have lessened somewhat; it seems to be getting better with time. I could hardly function at all before, but now I am working with people who have PTSD, and I am functioning on a much higher plane than I was.

My wife does an excellent job, helping and supporting me. If I am angry, she won't push. If she knows that I am having difficulties—she can sort of tell when my mind wanders and I'm upset because of my body language—then she'll avoid confrontation.

Well, I'm existing. I know I'm not happy, but I know I'll never be what I was before anyhow. I can function well enough, but as far as the future goes, I'm not looking for anything great to happen. I'm fifty-six now, so I put in my time. I don't have any ambitions to travel or anything like that when I retire. I have no idea what I'm going to do with myself to manage all the free time I'll then have. I'll deal with that when it comes to it.

People Ask Me
Where My Smile Went

Sergeant Doyle served in the U.S. Marine Corps from 1961 to 1969 as a machine gunner.

Forty years ago, when I was twenty-three, I was deployed to Vietnam: being in a continuous state of combat readiness, going on combat patrols during the day, experiencing ambushes at night, and having a constant fear of rocket attacks were the cause of my PTSD. I almost felt like in a trance during these times.

First I developed anxiety and alcohol dependency. I started withdrawing into myself and having a hard time relating to reality or making friends. I got and get mad or irritable very easily, for example, if someone disagrees with me. I had nightmares for years, and fireworks or loud noises would make me flinch or hit the deck. I used to wake up screaming, and my wife would ask me what's wrong. It became hard for my family to live with me, as I was constantly lashing out. I caused an end to my first marriage of twelve years. I gave up alcohol after ten years and remarried, and it's been a struggle for twenty-five years.

After eight years in the Marine Corps, I got out because I didn't want any more combat. I couldn't hold a job. I didn't like the people and thought they were out to get me. I would actually hate to go to work. Still today, I am antisocial, suffer from anxiety, and can't cope around people. Some people seem to rub me the wrong way and make me want to just shut them up and get them away from me. Sometimes I do feel emotionally numb and don't give a shit about anything or anyone. I am also suffering from depression. People ask me where my smile went and wonder why I don't smile anymore.

Actually, I like to see war movies, but I easily get really emotional. I try to avoid seeing violent death, such as people getting blown up or shot. A lot of times my reality is just shutting off the rest of the world and withdrawing into a world that is to my liking, such as being around my family even though there is no communication, just that they are there where I can see them out of harm's way.

The time I spend with my grandson is the only situation that is not influenced by my PTSD.

At first, I didn't really know what was wrong until I got a computer, went online, and chatted with fellow vets with the same problems. I applied for veterans' benefits, and they sent me to an impartial psychiatrist, who diagnosed PTSD in 2003, thirty-seven years after the traumatic events. I also have diabetes and all that goes with being exposed to Agent Orange. My PTSD symptoms have been getting worse. So, in 2007, I signed up for a three-year treatment program at a veterans' hospital and am now going to therapy. Talking to a psychiatrist and a therapist seems to be helping, also being on an antidepressant called Fluoxetine. As for my family, the best support they can give me is to be there for me and to try to understand.

I hope to get my life back.

We Walked Around on Eggshells

S. S.'s partner served in the Canadian army from 1984 to 2005.

I did not know my partner before the operational stress injury occurred, but he told me about the problem shortly after I got to know him in 2004. He had been diagnosed with PTSD in 2000 and said he mostly stayed at home for the four years before I met him. During that time, he went to a psychologist, tried antidepressants, physiotherapy, acupuncture, massage—and nothing helped him.

At first I didn't really notice that there was anything wrong with him until I moved in with him and Christmas came. He sort of withdrew from everything. He sat for days on the couch, watching TV. He is retired but only forty-five. He looked awful and didn't talk to anyone. He said he was in pain, and it had nothing to do with us. But he didn't say this until months later when we actually talked about it. I didn't know what was going on. I knew about the PTSD but didn't really understand.

I don't know what has caused his PTSD. He cannot talk about it and never has. I only know it was in Bosnia and had to do with children. The traumatizing event had happened around Christmas, but it seems that many other things happened then as well. Christmas seems to be a trigger for him. It's also around this time that troops are being deployed overseas.

After learning about PTSD, I tried to be careful around him so I wouldn't upset him. When that happened or he got into his funk, I felt like I was doing everything wrong—making too much noise, not making supper right or on time—or my kids were annoying him. We all kind of walked around on eggshells. His son finds him difficult to live with and moved out as soon as he could. When he was home, he stayed in his room most of the time or went out. My kids are old enough to deal with the situation if they don't take his mood to heart. He is much easier on them. My son moved out as well but not really because of him. Now it's only me and my daughter at home. She handles it fine. She just laughs and jokes with him, and he is okay with it. I try really hard to not put the blame on myself and give him space to get himself out of his mood. Sometimes, if we go out to see friends, he will forget himself and feel a little better.

He complains about himself. He finds it very difficult to think things through when he is fixing or building things. He says he can't focus, and it takes him a long time to do simple things that were easy in the past. He has too much pain to do the sports he did before because of physical injuries, and that frustrates and depresses him. He doesn't go out much and is mostly a homebody until spring, when he can get on his motorcycle and ride. That is one of the most important things that he seems to live for. So I encourage him.

Mostly it's months of depression, sleeplessness, times of being short-tempered, and rage that sometimes comes—he works very hard at keeping it under control at all times, though. He also works and works relentlessly until he drops, and then he can't move for weeks because he is in so much pain. I am not sure if his jealousy outbursts were part of his nature or if it was intensified because of the PTSD. Some of it was pretty ugly. He has frightened me. There aren't any outbursts anymore since I talked to him and told him I couldn't be with him if it continued. But the depression still comes after Christmas, and he just isn't approachable. He won't get help. He has stopped seeing the psychologist and will not take drugs because he doesn't trust the effects they have on him.

His depression, irritability, and pain are the most difficult aspects for us because there isn't anything we can do for him except leave him alone. He doesn't really want to talk about it unless it's to one of the guys like him.

I often feel hopeless. He isn't the same as when I met him. Maybe he just can't keep up the face he put on for me that first few months. It isn't easy to live with. I know he isn't nearly as affected as some of the other guys, but I wonder if I can handle it. Unfortunately I am not as strong as I should be for him, and I need support sometimes too. He cannot be that for me. He cannot handle that. I wish it could be different. It isn't what I thought it would be when we first got together.

I go to the family support meeting and have these friends to call when I need them. My old friends really don't understand and wonder why I stay. I try to take care of myself and give him his time to get himself back together. When my insecurities come up, I try to remember it's not me that is bothering him, that I can only help in some ways, but I can't fix it for him. It helps to know that others have these problems, many more serious than we do. It helps a lot to know some of what PTSD does to him so I can be more understanding.

My Life Has Been Ruined

Andrew served in the Royal Australian Air Force as a supplier in logistics and air movements from 1980 to 2003. He was in Somalia as part of the United Nations.

Serving in Somalia meant traumatic events on a daily basis: witnessing killing, seeing extreme poverty, being shot at and afraid for my own life. I started having nightmares and thus a lack of sleep. I began suffering from flashbacks and stress, felt a lot of anger in me, and started withdrawing from society. I knew I had a problem but didn't understand the symptoms until I spoke to other people and things fell into place: the chaplain at the base was talking to me one day and started asking some questions. He had dealt with a few guys that had returned form Somalia, and I think he may have had PTSD himself. He suggested I go to the Vietnam Veterans Counseling Service and speak with someone.

There I was diagnosed with PTSD in 1997, about three years after I had returned from Somalia.

I didn't meet any others suffering from PTSD for a few years after I was diagnosed and never realized there were so many with the same problems. It was not until my wife started looking for help for me that we discovered there were others going through exactly the same.

I went outside the system to find help and did not tell the military for several years. The positions I had held allowed me to hide the problem, but then I was put in a position where I was risking people's lives, and they started to see me making bad decisions. So I had to tell the military. The day I did was the day I went on sick leave. I was medically discharged with PTSD in 2003.

I was in Somalia twelve years ago when I was thirty-four. My life has been ruined:

I was outgoing and fun-loving. Now, I have no interest in any former hobbies, and I have strained relationships with my family, as I have withdrawn emotionally. I do not socialize very much at all and have become a recluse. I withdraw because it is easier than dealing with people. Sometimes I feel as if people are judging me.

I do not like to be in crowded situations—I like to be able to leave when I want to. My mood can change suddenly, and I don't like to be around people when this happens.

I get frustrated with queues and when people can't answer simple questions—I cannot tolerate fools. I get very annoyed with inconsiderate drivers and suffer from road rage. I can get angry at my wife and daughters for no reason. I tend to leave the situation before violence occurs.

I saw a lot of women get abused whilst overseas, and I could do nothing about it. Seeing or hearing of women being abused and mistreated here makes me very angry; I feel like I want to save them, protect them. My wife tells me I can't protect them all and that often it is not my business. She is right, but it feels so wrong not to do anything.

Flashbacks can occur at any time, especially if I am lying down, relaxing, or if a car backfires, or someone at a party lets off the small poppers, or when I'm at a show, and they suddenly use fireworks.

I have taken risks with my life I should not have; I have done stupid things that I know are dangerous. Without concern for myself or anyone else on the road, I have put my motorbike, a Honda Gold Wing, on cruise control and stood up with my arms stretched out to the side for a long distance. I have ridden very close to the wheels of semitrailers and raced through red lights. I was into self-mutilation and would do things like wash the concrete with acid without using gloves. I have attempted suicide on several occasions by taking too much medication and cutting my wrists.

I still suffer from all of the PTSD symptoms that I developed in the beginning. The majority even got more severe over time. Now, the severity of the symptoms depends on outside influences.

There was a time when my PTSD was getting better though. I had done a PTSD course at the hospital and was taking less medication. Then something else happened in my life that caused stress, and I sunk right back down again.

In addition to PTSD, I suffer from depression, an irritable bowel, and anxiety. I also have cardiomyopathy, caused by an overdose of psychiatric drugs given to me in the first hospital.

I have not been able to work because of my condition for three years now, and I am only forty-six years old. My outlook on my life and future is very dim.

People who have no understanding of PTSD can make wrong judgments. I've frequently experienced that when others learn about it, they then avoid you and disappear from your life, as if they think they can catch it or that you are a psychopath.

My family all knows a lot about PTSD, as my wife did lots of research and made sure the girls were always informed truthfully about my condition. My family is my best support, with maybe three close friends, two of whom have PTSD too. Often all I need is someone to talk to. I know I can talk to my family and friends without being judged, and that's enough at the moment.

Many Thought His PTSD Was Bullshit

D. R. is married to Andrew from the previous story.

∼

When my husband came home, I at first thought the changes in him were just a readjusting to family life: I had built a house while he was away, and we moved into it only a few weeks after his return. He worked like a madman—he had to have everything completed and finished in case something happened. I don't know what, just in case something happened. He seemed a bit distant, but things were generally good.

About three years later we moved interstate. The chaplain at the base was chatting to him one day and suggested he speak with a counselor at the Vietnam Veterans Counseling Service. They told my husband he had PTSD, and he informed me about this a few weeks later.

At first the chaplain did have to persuade my husband to seek help. He then saw a counselor, but he would not take any drugs. When we were moved to the east coast of Australia, he did not want to continue seeing anyone. Things went downhill, and I had to convince him to see a doctor. It was very difficult since he did not want the Defence Force to know of his condition, as it would mean a medical discharge. He was placed in a management position that was high stress, and things started to fall apart. I knew if he didn't get help, he would hurt himself or one of his troops.

My husband became withdrawn and antisocial. He hated going anywhere where a lot of people might be, he stopped going to sport events with the kids, and we stopped going out. He did not want to do anything. He could not shake hands with anyone, as his palms were always sweaty, and he was conscious of this. He suffered from severe depression all the time. He could not sleep and had nightmares. He has a hard time concentrating for a long period and has become obsessive compulsive about some things.

One time he tried to cut his wrists, not to commit suicide, I think, but to prove a point to someone or to get attention. He then went into a rage about it all and yelled at our children and told them it was their fault that he tried to do this. It was very unfair. He has never hit me or the kids—this was the worst he did. They were scared that day.

When I found out that my husband was suffering from PTSD, I first attempted to help him by just trying to understand. I did a lot of research on the Internet in order to learn about the condition. I wanted to be there for him.

Now I just give him the time he needs when he needs it. I work part-time in a flexible job and have been lucky that I have always been able to get flexible jobs since he's been suffering from PTSD. Sometimes he wants me to meet him somewhere for coffee, other times he needs me to talk to, but then does not say much.

We have lost touch with many people that were once considered good friends: they stopped visiting or calling. Many thought his PTSD was bullshit and he should just get over it. They thought he was weak. There are a few who are understanding, and these people have been wonderful.

My husband kept his PTSD from his family for years—they had no idea. It was easy to keep from them, though, as they were living in a different state.

I believe that I have developed some of the symptoms of PTSD myself. I need to be wanted and loved, and although I know that he really does love me, it is hard when it is never shown. His depression and not wanting to socialize with people is also a big burden on the family. Our children have been told about their father's condition from the beginning. Of course it affects them, but we try to give them as normal a life as possible. They still have friends over, and he is there for them when he can be. They can read him now and know when they can't approach him. It is a shame he can't go to some of their functions, but they understand this even though it still hurts them. They tell some of their friends about his PTSD, and although it is very hard when they tell their friends that Dad is in the mental hospital, we as a family realize that it could be worse: he could be out spending all the money drinking and gambling or being like some of their friends' dads, who beat them and their mums up.

I work with veterans on a daily basis, and this helps me. It also helps me to help others in the same situation. We are honest with it now, and if people choose not to like us for this, then that is their choice. We are not ashamed of it—it is a disorder, not a disease that people can catch. If my husband came home and said he had cancer, I would support him too, as would our family. My marriage vows say "for better or worse and in sickness and in health," and they mean a lot to me.

The government gives me a payment of ninety-five Australian dollars a fortnight for looking after my husband. I put this in a separate bank account, and once a year I take myself and one of the kids on a holiday. We usually go to Bali or Thailand for a week—this is our respite.

At Some Point the Soul Forms a Shield

Björn served from 1996 to 2000 as a paratrooper in the infantry of the German army.

I was twenty-three years old when I was deployed to the Kosovo eight years ago. I had already been to Bosnia in 1997, but what was going on down there in 1999 could in no way be compared to my deployment in 1997.

The war was over, and armistice had just been signed. We were sent there that same day to ensure the orderly withdrawal of the Serbs, which meant to safeguard the roads as far as possible and have them cleared so the Germans could advance with their ground forces. Naturally, the Serbs were not thrilled about having lost the war and behaved accordingly. The whole deployment was traumatizing. I saw corpses lying everywhere—in houses, in forests, and along roadsides; they were not being buried. We took care that everything was cataloged and that the dead were removed.

During a shooting, we returned fire and the Serbian soldiers died as a result of it.

In situations during which you have to return fire, you are full of adrenaline. You simply react—the way you were taught. Afterwards all the tension and strain, all the load, drops off your body, and you start shaking and breaking out in sweat—these are, after all, not everyday situations.

You actually don't talk with your comrades about it. You keep it to yourself. On top of it, there are constantly new impressions. And, at some point, the soul forms a shield—like callus on the skin: you block everything off and switch off inside. You have accepted the situation and are emotionally prepared that if you get hit—as hard as it may sound—you get hit.

In Bosnia, I started smoking. I had never smoked before—none of my family ever did. At some point I thought, well, so I'm smoking now, who cares. What I want to say with this is that the threshold was crossed. I took this attitude back home with me. I was no longer able to break through the shield and say, "Okay, you are home now, in civilian life, and everything is as before." I continued on this self-destructive trip. I started to drink extremely hard and to experiment with drugs. I just said to myself, that's how it is, and so what if I should bite the dust? It doesn't interest anybody anyhow. That was my attitude. I didn't get my grief off my chest since I didn't want to burden my parents with it. I felt this was my battle and no one else's.

I could no longer listen to certain CDs since I associated specific images from my deployment with them. I had sleeping disorders and was restless and nervous. My parents told me afterwards that they had also noticed that I was easily irritable.

For a short period I was in psychological treatment with a civilian psychologist. However, he didn't get to the point but tried to dig around in my family and my childhood. After a few sessions I said good-bye, "This was nice, I am healed," since it didn't bring anything.

When I was driving my car and got into a traffic congestion or had to stop at a red light, I used to have flashbacks: all of a sudden, images appeared before my eyes, and I was "caught" in a specific traumatizing situation from my deployment. My heartbeat accelerated greatly, and I broke out in a cold sweat. However, at that time I thought these symptoms appeared because I was taking a lot of cocaine and smoked a little weed.

The images from my deployment probably appeared during traffic jams or at red lights because I then switched off mentally for a moment—the specific situation itself didn't remind me of it. The images I "saw" were, for example, from the gunfight or the incident with the Serbian couple: an older Serbian couple had been living in the Kosovo for ages, and after the war, they were constantly threatened by Kosovo-Albanians who wanted them to leave and go back to where they came from. But they strictly refused. We had established some contact with this couple. You just feel drawn toward somebody, and the old woman had always reminded me of my own grandmother. One day, we had just completed our patrol round and were having coffee at the marketplace when the old man came to us and said he wanted to go home and saw that the door had been broken open. He had called to his wife, but she had not answered. He asked us to come with him because he was scared to enter the house. We did and found the old woman—beaten to death with an ax.

This was, of course, a very drastic situation for me, and when I was back home, I broke off all contact to my grandmother. My grandmother had actually brought me up to a large part since my parents had both been working, but after my deployment, I was no longer able to even sit at the table with her. She became very ill and had to go to an old people's home, and I didn't pay any attention to her anymore, just pushed her away. I didn't even go to her funeral. I was very hard that time, and I still regret it a lot. My parents were very disappointed. However, through the conversations that we had about my PTSD a while back, they were able to comprehend and understand.

My personality had changed after my deployment: I became very aggressive and stubborn. I was constantly mad about something and didn't avoid situations which involved fisticuffs—I actually enjoyed getting involved. My parents were shocked. I came home and did nothing but nag and yell. When there was a birthday party somewhere, I went there, got drunk, started a fight, and left—which I now feel really bad about. I felt like I was the greatest and let nobody get close to me. Meanwhile, my aggressiveness has lessened, and I'm no longer so stubborn—maybe because I have found some inner peace. I follow the news and what's going on in the world somewhat differently now. I have become more of a pacifist. I used to be convinced that our deployments were for the good and that I would have some impact, but in the end, I actually didn't achieve anything. Then you come home and get dropped like a hot potato. They packed us into a bus and drove us fifty men to the base chaplain. We were supposed to talk about our experiences while having coffee and cake, but of course, everybody just cracked jokes. You don't like to reveal your problems. You received your medal, and that was it. Of course, I also wanted to be a bit of a hero. I felt strong in front of my guys in the Kosovo and tried to show off a little at home. However, when I came back in 1999, I was actually nothing but a poor thing.

My civilian friends were all enjoying life and had girlfriends, while I was sitting at home in my room, got drunk, doped myself up—and this meant fulfillment for me. I broke off all contact to my friends, and I avoided crowds: I just couldn't take it if there were too many people around me or came close to me. I also gave up playing soccer. I wanted to have my freedom and just be worried about myself; I wanted to get everything over with as quickly as possible—let it all hang out one more time and then make the grand exit. I was serious.

But then I met my future wife. She was the first one that I talked to about my problems, and she simply listened. That took a load off my mind. And then I found out about the self-support group "Skarabäus." I had known the founding member, Captain S., already from before, when I was still working as a security guard at the academy of the medical service of the German armed forces. I had signed up there for six years after my discharge from the military. Captain S. was also at the academy, and we happened to get talking. He told me of Skarabäus, which was just getting started, and said that if I was having problems, I should drop by and we would try to find a solution. At first I thought that they were probably a bit screwy, but the captain kept approaching me, and finally I went to his house together with my wife. He explained to me that there were certain things my soul had not been able to handle and that were constantly burdening me now. For the first time, I heard the expression "posttraumatic stress disorder." We decided that we would frequently get together to talk. I didn't want to go to a psychologist or take medication. I wanted to try to get the situation under control by myself. Captain S. also asked me if I wouldn't prefer to do something else rather than constantly staring out of the window of the academy at night and thinking about my problems. I agreed, and he found me another job.

Now everything is looking up again: the symptoms, for example, the anxiety, have meanwhile lessened a bit, and I can sleep through again—probably because of the different demands at work, which put other thoughts in my mind. At the academy, where I had sat guard at the front for six years, I had never been able to switch off mentally: I constantly had to deal with young soldiers and was still integrated in military life; I only had changed my uniform. In my new job, I have found some self-fulfillment and am actually coming to life again. I'm concentrating on other things now and accept my situation as a matter of course, even though I still have a problem when I see news of the war in Afghanistan on TV and then remember how it was for me in the Kosovo.

I still can't take crowds. I don't feel comfortable when there are too many people around me, and I don't like taking public transportation. I prefer being alone in my personal surroundings.

Some people say, "Oh my God, what have you been through, what have you experienced? That is horrible." I can do without the sympathy. People can best help you by talking with you. Listening is important, maybe also approaching the person, not to be afraid, to simply say, "What's wrong? Tell me! Let's sit down and try to find a solution." Not to say, "Maybe he'll come on his own, we'll see how things develop." It took me years to come on my own, after I had almost ruined myself. My parents had always watched me and wondered if this would end well but never had enough courage to interfere. Now, years later, we talked about it for the first time, after everything had come to the surface again through Skarabäus and all those television reports a year ago. In the end they were able to understand. It was almost like drawing a line in order to start all over again.

I honestly have to admit, had I not met my wife, I would not be sitting here now. She and my new job have helped me most:

to meet new people, to just switch off, and draw a line under my military experience. I have safely packed away all the photos of my time in the service. I hardly ever look at them. This chapter is closed for me.

My hope for the future is to hold my job as long as possible, that we'll eventually have kids, and that we continue living the way we are now. The past is part of one's life—it cannot be undone. You simply have to accept the situation as it is. Life still has so many ups and downs waiting for everyone that you have to master somehow; if you survived what I have experienced, you can survive all other things too. Looking at it this way, my experience also has a positive aspect: I can overlook situations now, which many get irritated about. For example, if people get upset because things move too slowly at the cash register and they don't have time—that's just the way it is. It's not the end of the world. Or if people complain about the boss and that the pay is too low—you'll just have to put up with it. The most important thing is to have a job in the first place and to get paid, that's at least what I think. I look at things differently now. Everything is going better now.

I Long to Be Who I Was

Specialist A. L., a female veteran, served in the U.S. Army from September 2000 to August 2005 in supply.

Iraq 2003: About ten miles over the Iraq line, I encountered a hostile village while on convoy to Tikrit. During convoy, I was driving and hit a child. I remember feeling unsure, and everything slowed down. I moved the incident to the rear of my mind, and later it hit hard when the evidence was on the bumper of my Humvee. I remember feeling as if the whole thing were a dream and kind of foggy. I was shaky and emotional but close after just numb.

Later in my deployment a roadside firefight caused a traffic jam, and several people died in the street. I was not involved directly in firefight but witnessed the devastation. Later again, on convoy outside Tikrit, a contractor two vehicles ahead of us hit an IED and died. Grizzly sight, as he was not in a military armored vehicle.

While overseas I started participating in dangerous behavior. I would take unwanted missions to drive anywhere and everywhere. I wanted to clear houses and do convoys. Guns became very important. I started drinking to help me to sleep. I became verbally aggressive towards my superiors and uncontrollable. I did not tell anyone what had happened because of fear of persecution. Because I took on dangerous missions, my so-called symptoms were overlooked, and I was commended as a super-trooper sort of soldier. Mainly because there were only females working in direct line of supervision. To them, I didn't seem to be afraid of anything, but in reality I wanted to die like the boy.

Upon returning to the States the real problems started. Now I couldn't sleep as a result of nightmares, anxiety, and feelings as if someone was watching me or out to get me. During the day I was aggressive towards my kids, my husband, anyone who came into my path. I was experiencing flashbacks, but the army had told me that I would.

The very first episode was when my parents came down to visit, and we went to the San Antonio river walk. It grew dark while we were there, and I became irrational. I felt that everyone was an enemy and felt helpless without a weapon. I became emotional and feared being shot from the tallest buildings. My parents were horrified, my kids were upset, my husband was worried. It was very traumatic for me, as I was confused and extremely embarrassed. I was shortly thereafter sent to a new assignment in South Carolina. At that unit even more problems surfaced. My husband and I were not intimate. I cut off feelings for my kids and parents. I felt isolated from all friends still left in Iraq. I longed for people that understood . . . I kept all the dreams and feelings from everyone and wouldn't open up to new people at all. I was hardly sleeping as the face I had seen in my dreams horrified me. The face of the little boy. . . . His facial expression as I was coming at him still haunts me. At this new unit the company sergeant major was my "enemy" from day one. She stayed on me about weight guidelines, which I didn't comply with because with all the depression, I just didn't feel like doing anything. I felt there was no one that understood since all of the soldiers there had stayed stateside, none of them had been to the war.

As time passed, eventually my husband and I agreed on drive-through sex—which was my rule: no kissing, no hugging, just sex.

I got into trouble after a trip to the local flea market when I almost attacked a vendor for being rude to one of my children. As the symptoms escalated, my life quality was deteriorating. And I didn't understand what was wrong with me. I was skittish when driving, would completely freak out at the sound of gunfire, or a car backfiring, or fireworks. I was rude, shy, callous, and cold. In the end I was not only suicidal but homicidal, confused, depressed, and had no future in my eyes.

Being homicidal, I had gone to the company chaplain about my hostilities towards the company sergeant major, and the feeling that she was out to get me. I told him that I was having some disturbing and violent dreams about her. He laughed me off and told me to exercise. A few months later, we got a new commanding officer in my unit. His wife had been to Iraq, and one day he e-mailed me a survey that asked a lot of questions. In his e-mail he asked if I was experiencing any of these symptoms. As I was reading through, I started to cry, and I replied to him, "Yes, Sir, every day of my life." He wrote back almost immediately and said to come see him now.

It is important to note that this captain was extremely kind and attentive. He made me feel that he had my best interests at heart. The interview was in no way threatening to my career. The way he approached the subject was key because the staff sergeant that was over me had attempted to talk to me several times, and I felt he should mind his own damned business, and I think I told him to stay out of my personal life. Anyway, this captain told me that everything that we discussed was off record, and for the first time in a long time I felt safe. He had told me that he had been watching me and that he was concerned, that he had spoken with his wife about me, and she suggested the survey. He asked me what was going on, and with his office door closed, I broke down. I told him about all of my feelings. We did not go into detail about the events in Iraq but talked more on the level of where I was at that time. I told him about my plans to kill the company sergeant major, and he was understanding of my feelings. He said he knew that she had mistreated me. At that point he asked me to go see a psychologist, but he said it was voluntary, that he would make the call. I did go see the psychologist, and he kept the entire thing completely confidential. I don't know if I would be where I am today if someone had not said, "Hey, I care, and this is what you need to do." That is why I go to the vet chat rooms; they may not have someone like that in their lives.

I was still in the army when I was diagnosed with PTSD. My commanding officer had referred me to mental health, where I had one appointment, and then I was assessed by a psychiatrist. This was one year and six months since I had returned from Iraq. At the second visit he diagnosed me and put me on Zoloft. I went to see him twice a week for a month, and then we cut back to once a week till I got out in August 2005. I was also referred to a psychologist, a caseworker, with whom I did the talking and working out. I only saw the psychiatrist at the case-worker's recommendation if I was out of meds or if she thought I should increase them.

Luckily I was in a nondeployment unit, but I do know that my career changed. I was not allowed by command to have a weapon. The commander protected me from situations that might result in an episode, that is, field environments that simulated combat or rifle ranges.

I was always a social person—outgoing and full of energy. I had a lot of self-esteem and was very friendly. Since I've been suffering from PTSD, I can be very introverted. I don't like crowds, I have trust issues, and I tend to be suspicious of everything. Driving, crowds, movies, fireworks, Iraqi news all make me feel weird. I feel ashamed of not being able to control it. I don't feel free anymore, I feel afraid of life.

I had a substance abuse problem with NyQuil and alcohol, I struggle with depression, but it does get better. I fight aggression issues. I think all of these things are the fallout of having PTSD.

I would say intelligence and technical abilities are not influenced by PTSD, but I can't think of anything socially that is not influenced.

I know that before and during treatment I personally stayed in arguments. I would take most everything personal. If someone made remarks about the job I was doing or said something to my kids or even made a comment about the war, I would take it as fighting words. Before I was a laid-back kind of person. I feel that I am on my way to being that way again, but . . . I have to fight the urge. I know that when I drink I am ready to fight. My opinion is that someone suffering from PTSD has issues of guilt and anger that probably never will completely disappear. In a way they want to punish themselves for the things that have happened. Most of the time you look back and wonder what you could have done, or you hold a lot of resentment towards a type of person, that is, ethnicity or a personality trait. I think being a vet also gives you a feeling of special treatment in that you feel the average citizen doesn't measure up to what you have seen, done, or experienced, and you feel that you deserve more respect than average. Like you have earned it.

In my own experience I attacked a lady at the flea market for asking my kids not to touch the toys in her booth. However, she was rather rude, and I felt she disrespected them and me. I was enraged almost immediately and voiced my anger; she retaliated with words, and the situation got way out of hand. I tried to get to her and was shouting obscenities and threatening her publicly, and my husband held me back. I was extremely angry, and I know in my heart that if I had gotten to her, she would have been badly hurt. When something like that happens to me, it's like I focus on that one person, and everything fades away, and I want to take all the frustrations and anger and hurt out on the target. It looks like a bull's-eye to me, and aggression is a channel for releasing all those feelings that you can't get out otherwise. It's like the sound of glass breaking—you can't explain why it helps, but it does. Aggression also gives power to those who don't feel powerful. If you argue or hit, it immediately puts you in the power place, and the rest of the time the PTSD has the power. It has the control, so I guess in a way it's a way to feel whole again. Then you feel bad, and it starts to build, and the cycle goes on.

On numerous occasions I was hard to get along with and stayed on the proverbial soapbox about something all the time. If someone within my path was in the way, I would just remove them. All of this is not in my nature. My kids were afraid of me and what I was capable of, and I feared myself—I was not sure what I was doing or why.

When people ask me, "How was it? Over there?" it infuriates me. I understand their curiosity, but I also resent the implication that it was anything other than hell. I find it disrespectful of them to ask a question that opens up such a can of worms. I fight the urge to tell them exactly what I think of people that ask that question. Sometimes I feel like giving them what they are asking for—if they think it's a game, then tell them the gory details. I say this because it took me over a year to tell my mom that I was diagnosed with PTSD. After a couple of months of probing she finally said, "Well, what exactly happened," and I just went the hell off. I told her, and I gave her what she wanted, and she was speechless. Oh, I paid for it with over a week of nightmares and flashbacks. You see, talking in detail about such things brings back so much. But hell, the look on her face told me she won't do that again.

In my experience, because I am a woman, I feel that people think I was sheltered from the real war. Especially men in the military. That is a preconceived notion that couldn't be further from the truth. That pisses me off and brings up rage when I encounter a man that says something like that.

PTSD almost ruined my life. I almost lost my husband, my children, my career, my mind. I had no desire for any social interaction. I feel stupid a lot because of the failure to concentrate or focus on things. And when things happen, I feel embarrassed. I feel like less of a person sometimes. Like an outcast. It's hard to remember that all of these feelings are internal, and others don't readily see. I long to be who I was, and it is hard to come to terms with the fact that that may never happen.

The moment a name was put on what I was experiencing, I started to heal and learn everything I could about how to beat it. Before I was diagnosed, I just thought I was crazy, and I would keep inside out of fear someone would figure it out. Once I felt safe, then I started to talk and let out those fears. The medication helped, and when I could sleep, it was easier to focus. I started to draw pictures of the event and just cry and keep a journal. Improvements were apparent after the medication and sleep.

My husband could be the poster boy for how to help with PTSD. This has been a long, drawn-out struggle. He has been attentive and understanding—even when he didn't understand. He would listen and not judge. He would not tell my business to everyone. He was constantly reassuring me that things were okay and he was there. He gave me freedom and stability at the same time. However, my mother was critical and intrusive and belittled what I felt. She was no help at all.

Zoloft, counseling, sleep, support from my husband, and the trust of my counselor all led to this improvement.

I was thirty-one years old at the time of the traumatic incident. Three and a half years have passed.

Today I have learned to live with some things. I have learned to evade others, and some I have healed. With the sleeping pills, the dreams come only occasionally. I tend to try to isolate myself and have mood swings. My mind wanders frequently, and I still have problems with focusing. I can't handle movies that have extreme violence or war scenarios. I still have trouble talking about the war, but I have the desire to do so. My family life is better, I am not abusive. My husband and I are happy and intimate. I have reconnected with my children. I am not homicidal or suicidal. When I have had a bad day, I have the urge to drink. I have bouts of depression, but it's not constant. When I drive, sometimes I worry that something bad will happen, and I tend to flash back at familiar sights of Iraq like small trees, or dowdy colored homes, or certain geographical resemblances. Loud noises still tend to cause a rapid heartbeat and flashbacks or bad dreams, but they are expected now. I understand that what I experience has a name and some of the symptoms may never disappear, but things are a whole lot better now.

The aggressive nature of it all, the hate inside of me has lessened as I understand more of what is going on. Just knowing that PTSD is real lets me know that I wasn't going crazy. With sleep aids I can sleep, sometimes even without the sleeping pills. Zoloft helps me to stay focused and calm. The feelings of resentment towards Iraqi people have decreased; the anger for myself has decreased. The IED incident was the first to fall into the background. I still feel like a paper bag or a can on the highway could kill me sometimes, but I don't think of the contractor every day. I hear voices almost daily and see things out of the corner of my eye. My ears ring, but I don't think that is from PTSD. The voices have come later, but I do notice that a hard day brings symptoms out.

Some days are better than others—you just got to deal with it.

My outlook on life is positive. I think things happen in our lives that aren't foreseeable, and whether it's a wreck or a bad childhood or war, you got to deal with the fallout. I see PTSD affecting me for the rest of my life. I will probably be on medication and have issues, but I see me taking note of what it is and living life. I think a person's attitude towards what happens is extremely important, it determines defeat or success. I feel that I spent enough time in the dark, and I don't want to ever go back. I know that episodes and symptoms will come and go, and I will be up and down on the emotional roller coaster, but unlike many of my comrades, I am here to tell the story, and that in itself is a blessing. So, what right do I have to complain?

My outlook will depend on the day and what has happened, but at night, when things are silent, I have to remind myself that no matter the dream, I am not there anymore, and when morning comes, the echoes are only a memory.

I Had Planned
to Have Myself Shot

Warrant Officer André served in the Canadian Land Forces from 1975 to 2006 as a vehicle technician.

❦

Four distinct events were the cause of my PTSD:

My first traumatic event happened at the age of about fourteen at the Base Valcartier Cadet camp thirty-three years ago. There I witnessed a grenade explosion, which killed six cadets. I was in utter shock and disbelief of the carnage that was unfolding before my eyes. It caused intense fright in the days that followed.

I was shot at in the winter of 1981/1982 in Cyprus during a UN peace mission. Being shot at without the possibility of shooting back was very frightening and surreal.

Another time I saw an armored vehicle accident during a training exercise, in which three vehicles crashed into each other, causing serious injuries to about ten troops. The overwhelming sight and sounds of the wounded troops that we removed from the wreckage strongly affected me, and I had my first flashback of the grenade incident. On another occasion, an unexploded ordnance (UXO) was found in a case of artifacts. Everything went well during the incident, but afterwards I experienced a whole range of emotions—rage, hostility, fright—and I was ready to kill whoever had done this. There were also flashbacks and bad dreams of the grenade incident.

I was able to deal very well with every event individually and even collectively. I told myself that whatever happened was part of the job and therefore normal. The symptoms were few and short lived. I seemed to be able to overcome the traumatic experiences and cope with them without any negative effects. I was to find out in late 2004, however, that I had not been able to deal with the events at all. I had simply pushed them aside and ignored them. I was forced to admit to myself that I had a serious problem in August 2004 in Haiti after a failed suicide attempt— my own! I was part of a team that was closing the Canadian mission in Haiti. I awoke one day to the sound of gunfire outside the wire. That sound, that smell, brought everything back with a vengeance: the screaming and the kids wounded by the grenade, the distinct sound of incoming gun fire in 1982, and the moans and complaints of the injured troops caught in the armored vehicle pileup. It was too much, and I lost it. I planned to have myself shot by a Brazilian UN contingent troop. My plan failed because I was not able to shoot the first round. That was my wake-up call—I really, really needed help. Once back in Canada after the mission, I sought help from the mental health section of our medical clinic.

As of August 2004, I had not been able to function properly in my old work environment anymore. I could not concentrate on my work, I withdrew from my coworkers, could not meet deadlines for reports, etcetera. It was like life had been sucked out of me. I had become an empty shell, a shadow. I was already separated from my wife, my children had left home to study in another city, and I lacked any family support. During my therapy after the Haiti mission I was alone, scared, and ready to end it all once again because life for me was nothing but a dead end. Nothing interested me anymore, even the activities I once enjoyed meant nothing to me anymore. I had no social life whatsoever.

I was diagnosed with depression in 2000. My PTSD diagnosis came in 2004—twenty-nine years after the first traumatic event. It has been an uphill battle ever since. I have thought of suicide many times, I have bouts with survivor guilt, the good old "why them and not me" question. I have had many nightmares concerning my traumas and a sleeping disorder. Though many have sleepless nights, I, on the contrary, can sleep up to sixteen hours a day. I am extremely vigilant of my surroundings and trust very few people.

I have developed a high sensitivity level for death in general. Animal carcasses on the side of the road will really affect me in a negative way. News footage of Afghanistan and Iraq is very disturbing for me. Just now, six Canadian soldiers were killed by a roadside bomb in Afghanistan—another six boys who are going back home in pieces.

The PTSD and the depression have taken over my everyday life. There are good days and bad days. Often I have difficulties making day-to-day decisions since I have very limited confidence in myself and therefore second-guess myself constantly. Also, my concentration has been severely affected. My personality has not changed. I am not aggressive or abusive. I do not drink at all, and I do not have a drug or substance abuse problem.

After the formal PTSD diagnosis I remained in the forces for about two more years. They accommodated me, took me off all training, and assigned me to other administrative tasks. I was released from the forces in October 2006.

I have been in therapy since 2005, and things are getting better. I have a long way to go before returning to the person I was. The intense thoughts of suicide have almost disappeared, and I have started to enjoy life once again. I have a wonderful and understanding woman in my life at the present, and things are looking up. The future is not always all black.

Therapy, medication, and social support have all helped me. There is no miracle pill that will take away the pain of PTSD. The doctors can only help you if you want to help yourself. And there are only a few friends who have any idea of what a person who suffers from PTSD is going through. Family can help only to a certain point. Only someone who has had the same types of trauma can understand what it feels like to have PTSD. Therefore, other soldiers, police, and fire department personnel and other high-risk-job employees are a good source of comfort and understanding.

Some days, life is worth living to the fullest. Other days, life sucks, and I wonder, what am I still doing here on earth? Fortunately, there are more good days than bad.

Every Day Is a Struggle

Bunnie's husband Kevin has been in the military for twenty-four years, serving since 1984. A petty officer first class in interior communications in the U.S. Navy after six years of active duty and one year in the reserves, he later reenlisted in the U.S. Army National Guard, where he currently serves with the infantry as a staff sergeant.

Kevin was given two weeks' leave at the end of January 2005 during his tour in Iraq to come home. During this time I began noticing things like sleepwalking, terrible night sweats, nightmares, and talking in his sleep about blowing things up, dead bodies, bodies on fire, etcetera. He had panic attacks and a fear of driving or riding in our car when another car "rolled up on us," as he put it. I also noticed his lack of concentration.

I began asking questions like "Hey buddy, did you have a nightmare last night because you said this or did that?" I also asked him if he would feel more comfortable being in the driver's seat and, if so, why. Kevin, however, had only two replies to my questions and concerns: he would either just look at me with a blank stare or get very angry and have violent outbursts. I told him about how badly he was sweating in his sleep and that maybe he should see a doctor. This particular time he asked me what he was saying in his sleep: it was something about sector 4 and an IED, something about searching a house in that sector, and he was yelling for his men to "get down." He said that this nightmare was not unlike all the others; actually it was just another night in Iraq for him.

While he was home for those two weeks, we talked a lot about what was happening to him over there and exactly what his unit was doing. Once, when he was out on patrol, a sniper shot one of the guys straight through his helmet in front of him, his men, and a group of kids. During his leave, my husband had continuous nightmares about that incident. There were many more; some Kevin will not talk to me about. These are just a few he has told me:

When a "bad guy" gets shot and he is not from the province where he is killed, then the others who live there simply let the body lay and rot. It is sometimes used to hide explosives that are meant to kill our soldiers. My husband also said that kids are used as shields. He talked about being in his Bradley directly behind another one that ran over an IED and was blown up, and all you can do is watch your guys trapped inside, being burned to death while pieces are being blown up all around you and on your vehicle.

Kevin had returned from a deployment to Kosovo only nine months prior to leaving for Iraq. He, our children, and I had been in therapy since then because he was having similar problems that time but not to the magnitude he has now. While he was home on the two-week leave in January, he went to a session with us. About two months after the deployment was finally over, I started noticing changes in his behavior and sleep pattern again: as soon as he had to begin thinking seriously about returning to his civilian job and resume the responsibilities of husband, father, and supporter, he began to feel overloaded, and the signs slowly appeared. A few times he had panic attacks so bad that he thought he was dying or having a heart attack and asked me to take him to the hospital, which is so not like him. I suggested he go and talk to our family therapist. However, once he could feel that there was something wrong with him, he didn't want to go to any doctor anymore. He said he could handle it himself. It was almost as if he wanted to know, but once he continued to get closer to the real truth, he didn't want to know. . . .

Before my husband left for Iraq, he was employed as a corrections officer at a maximum-security prison. He was in great health and was an ambitious, hardworking man. When he came home, he had four to six weeks of leave before he had to return to work at the prison. He would have had the possibility to go back before this time was up but opted not to and waited until the very last day when he had no choice but to go. He went to work for one day, came home that night a total mess, and the very next day called to put in for an early retirement due to being unable to cope with the daily pressures.

Being there for Kevin was all I could do. Listening and trying to understand was a start. Eventually his behavior became too overwhelming even for me to deal with. He was sleeping almost every hour of every day and was not worried about even searching for a job; he was having devastating, violent outbursts of hatred and anger; and his panic attacks became weekly trips to the local hospital. He was doing things out of the "norm" and without thinking them through as far as consequences go, he was being distant and seemed not to care; he withdrew from our kids, grandkids, me, and work. Even everyday tasks were too much for him, and he would get frustrated and angry. Simply talking to him about normal everyday things that we would otherwise be taking care of together became a struggle and a heated argument. So, I had to get myself into the mind-set that all I can do is be here and try to deal with what I am going through in a manner that doesn't involve him. I decided to write letters to anyone who I thought might be able to help us, from politicians to the news media. I started digging deep and researched soldiers returning from Iraq, posttraumatic stress, depleted uranium poisoning, and other symptoms our soldiers are bringing home with them.

The strain on our family was outrageous: I was at the end of my rope, my cup was full, and I was having MS (multiple sclerosis) flare-ups due to the stress it was causing. We would get into tremendous arguments over the fact that he was having such a hard time. Our children began withdrawing, becoming depressed, and their habits changing. It took a lot of arguing, crying, and understanding on my part—I went from pleading and begging him to go to the doctor to demanding it.

Our family doctor diagnosed him with PTSD, just as our family therapist had done before.

Kevin was on medication, but since we had lost our insurance coverage after his retirement from his job at the prison, he was without psychotherapy, and things got progressively worse with each day. It took almost a year to get him into the VA. They too diagnosed him with PTSD. He now goes to the VA's PTSD clinic about once a month, and they prescribe his medication. He is taking Cymbalta, Lexapro, a few others for pain, and now also some for sinus problems from the dust and debris from explosions in Iraq. When Kevin comes home from the VA clinic, he is full of anger and rage, and it takes him days to get over it.

Kevin used to be very strong. He would do anything for anyone, but never would you know he needed any type of help—or, if you knew and wanted to do anything for him, he would refuse it. Having a job and being able to provide for us had always been his number one priority. He prided himself on being able to do that one thing and be the best at it that he could be. He would fix whatever went wrong and shield us from any harm. Now, he is unable to do any of that. He was out of work for over a year, and his determination to do anything has dwindled to almost nothing. He has lost interest in everything that once brought him pleasure. He is withdrawn and only does exactly what he has to do to be able to function but nothing else. He is now, in some strange way, "unreachable" and uncaring. He says that he doesn't have the energy to care about anyone or anything. I have to push him to do things with us and to take care of things that I am unable to, like shingles falling off our roof.

Kevin had tried to get unemployment when he returned from Iraq, but it was denied. After his early retirement from his job at the prison, it was months of him sleeping his life away and finding creative ways of making tasks around the house last longer than you could imagine, as well as an outrageous amount of excuses why he wasn't able to even look for work, let alone get a job. Finally, after countless fights over our drowning financial situation and the depletion of our savings, he began looking for work over the Internet. Friends, our pastor, and even our family doctor would call here with leads on jobs for him, and he would do nothing. Most days he wouldn't even get out of bed or bathe. It was horrible. Finally, I started giving him the phone when someone would call here for payment on his hospital bills or anything else. He would get *so* angry, but it brought him back to a tiny part of reality, and he began buying newspapers and looking for work. After about eight months he finally took a job with a contractor who needed an electrician for local steel mills. About three months into that job, the work slowed, and he was laid off. They told him to talk to another guy who ran a similar company and was looking for someone with Kevin's qualifications. However, Kevin wanted so much to be able to collect unemployment so he wouldn't have to get out of bed each day. Finally he got his wish but then was called for an interview at a company as an electrician. That job lasted him one month, and he was fired. He has never been fired from anything in his life! So, again he attempted unemployment, and it was granted. Then, about eight months ago, someone called who wanted Kevin to come in to talk about an electrician's position, and they hired him. Kevin forces himself each day to get out of bed and go to work so we do not lose our home—but that is all he can manage to do. He likes this job, though, and it is really going good there for him, thank God.

Kevin's PTSD diagnosis didn't have any consequences on his military career. His unit is also scheduled to return to Iraq again before his retirement date. Kevin is not the only soldier in his unit who has been diagnosed with PTSD and/or is on medication for it.

No one in our family or circle of friends treats Kevin any different than they did before he had PTSD. I believe it is because no one realizes the extent of what he is going through—or the kids and I for that fact. He works very hard to hide his symptoms to the point of seeming like a completely different person when he is around others outside our home. He doesn't want anyone to know how bad things are. It's like a "dirty little secret."

Kevin has good days and bad days, but when he has a bad day, it is a horrible time for every one of us:

One day, when he was hired to do electrical work at a local steel mill, he came home a little later than usual. I could tell that he seemed a bit more on edge than he normally is, but I didn't mention anything. The reason I do not bring up things to him is that it causes a major blow up, and he becomes so loud and angry that there is no controlling him or the situation once it reaches that point of no return. He and I started having a conversation; when our sixteen-year-old daughter mentioned something, he went off. He started screaming and cursing and told us to shut up and that he didn't care about anything or anyone. Our twelve-year-old son started crying and asked him to stop yelling, and Kevin actually looked at him and swore at him. He has never talked to our kids like that, and if he ever were anywhere and heard or saw someone talking to their kids that way, he would tell them about themselves. His screaming and yelling and cussing at us lasted about twenty minutes, then just as fast as it started, it stopped, and he went to bed. We were all devastated, and the next day he didn't even acknowledge what had happened or that he should be sorry. It was just another day to him. Meanwhile the kids and I were hurt and angry at his treatment and words. Two days later I was down in our cellar, putting wood in our burner, and he was chopping wood. We started talking about Iraq, and he told me then that when he left work two days prior, a worker was running a jackhammer. He said he had a flashback and thought he was being shot at. He jumped behind a dumpster and stayed there for thirty minutes. He said this was why he was late coming home, and I found out that it was the root for the blowup that day.

Another time Kevin was late getting home because a truck in front of him had a sheet of ice blow off his top and into the road. He had a flashback again, thinking that the truck in front of him had been blown up, and he ended up putting his truck into a ditch because of it. We had another big blowup that evening too.

When he starts yelling and screaming at us, all we can do is try to walk away and continuously ask him not to yell, but nothing helps. It is as if we just have to take it until he's finished, and then we have to forget it ever happened: we can't talk to him about it, as it would turn into a horrible event with hurt and scared feelings.

He does things that would often make you wonder what he was thinking to make him decide to do whatever he did because there is no logic behind it or reason for it. You cannot simply talk to him or ask him any questions about anything he is doing because he thinks you are questioning his reasons or that you are attacking him—as if he is not good enough or what he did or is doing is not good enough. You cannot disagree with him in even the slightest manner.

Kevin continues to suffer from panic attacks and night terrors, but they are not as bad as before. He still has night sweats, he sleepwalks, he has breathing problems and has to use oxygen while sleeping. However, he has not had any angry outbursts for over two months. He is depressed and finds it hard to function and stay on track to be able to complete normal daily routines. He hardly leaves the house, he barely spends time with our kids or grandkids, he hardly talks to me or our kids anymore, he goes to bed before 10 p.m. and gets up in the afternoon unless he has to go to work. Then he goes to work, comes home, goes to bed, gets up with enough time to get ready and leave for work, and repeats that everyday.

Our son is devastated by this because he adores his father. He used to spend lots of time with our son—now it is almost as if he has to be forced to spend time with him. Our son has become withdrawn and depressed and is always sad. Our daughter has also become withdrawn and avoids her dad whenever she can. I walk around our home as if I am afraid to upset him for fear I will be verbally abused, or he will start yelling and cussing at me over something I should've been able to avoid. His PTSD has traumatized me. But not just me: our kids are really lost in all of this. They are hurting, confused, and frightened. It is a daily struggle for both our kids and myself to remain able to understand that Dad is going through something really bad, and we have to try and help by understanding and being here for him. It is as if we waited eighteen months for Kevin to come home, so everything would be okay and we could be a family again. . . . And now he is home and things are worse than when he was in Iraq. We are fighting something we cannot see, and most times it feels as if it is a losing battle.

The worst is the fear. Fear that Kevin will never be able to get back to where he was before the deployment. Fear that our family won't be able to withstand all of this turmoil and destruction. Fear that Kevin may hurt himself or someone else because of his violent outbursts. Fear of not having enough support from our government and the VA. Fear of being alone in all of this. Fear of not knowing each morning when we wake if Kevin is going to have a good day or a bad day. Mostly it's the fear of not knowing if I will be strong enough to help our kids and Kevin through this—or myself for that matter. Without our faith in God, our family would have fallen apart a long time ago. I have to hold tight to the belief that God did not keep Kevin safe while he was in Iraq to bring him home and have his family or him fall apart. I believe that God has brought us this far and He will lead us to the end and place us exactly where He wants us to be—together, as a whole, as a family. That is not to say that every day isn't a struggle, because it is. But I know that without my faith I would be lost and completely devastated over everything.

Behind Locked Doors and with a Barbed Wire over the Fence

Private R. was a rifleman in the infantry of the Australian army and served from 1967 to 1969 in the National Service.

I was twenty when I went into the army as a conscript and twenty-two when I first experienced actual combat. That was almost thirty-eight years ago. More than one event caused my PTSD, but being fired upon and firing at the enemy while on patrol in South Vietnam was the main reason.

One incident happened when I was on sentry duty in the jungle: it was very hot and humid, and I had been stung badly by wasps the day before and was still feeling the effects of the poison in my guts. I was lying flat on my belly, underneath a leafy bush of some sort. I had been watching the track for an hour or so, and then, quite suddenly it seemed, a North Vietnamese soldier appeared, probably about ten or fifteen meters away. I remember shaking my head and thinking I might be seeing things but quickly realized that he was there, that he had stopped, and that he appeared to be listening and looking in the direction of where the rest of my group was. (They were about twenty-five meters behind me.) I aimed my M16 and fired a burst; almost instantly the NVA soldier fired back, his rounds disintegrating the leaves immediately above my head. I struggled to change magazines, thinking the NVA soldier was coming for me. I felt extreme fear, that I would die, that I was on my own—which I was while on sentry during the day.

On the same day, as with other contacts and incidents that occurred during my time as a rifleman in South Vietnam, I led our section—five including me—out to search for the NVA and whoever else might be around. During that time, as well as after other things that happened, which I won't talk about, I remember being unable to stop shaking, being super alert, expecting to die, feeling occasional nausea (but heat probably contributed there), being possibly in shock, but still doing my job.

I got physically ill ten years ago, and being so ill, I degenerated mentally. Until then I had tried not to think about my experiences by working long hours and involving myself in many sports and activities. Apart from the pain of memories about South Vietnam, we also had to deal with abuse and rejection from the community when we came back from the war due to it's unpopularity and the fact that it was clear that we—the U.S. and its allies—were not winning. I think the symptoms were always there but pushed into the background by constantly doing things so as not to think.

After my recovery from the 1997 illness, I realized I needed to do something, and a friend referred me to the Vietnam Veterans Federation. I was diagnosed with PTSD about thirty years after the traumatic events. I have also been diagnosed with anxiety and depression.

Still today, I experience hypervigilance, a fear and wariness of strangers, and I hate being out at night, particularly walking. I don't like to have my back to anyone, nor to doors or windows, especially in public places or in exposed positions outside. I am easily startled when, for example, someone walks behind me and I don't hear them, then see something move out of the corner of my eye. It brings on feelings of tension, nervousness, and alertness to danger; someone coming towards me even makes me edgy sometimes. Make that most of the time. I have barbed wire along my back fence, for Christ's sake!

I get panic attacks; I feel vulnerable and restless. I have sleep problems, wake up sweating, and have nightmares. Imagine what it's like to wake up in the middle of the night in a sweat, after reliving in your sleep the nights spent on patrol in remote lonely places, in the middle of seemingly nowhere, with darkness all around. It is quiet, but every noise, no matter how soft, serves to give you away. Or imagine to be woken by the sound of claymores and machine gun and rifle fire in the pitch blackness that is suddenly lit up by flares and tracers. For a split second you don't know where the hell you are, then fire into the night your own rifle. Then the weapons stop, and there is a new sound but one heard before: low moaning, somewhere out in the night. And it is black. Black until dawn. But you aren't there anymore; you are in your bed at home, nearly thirty years later. And this has happened before, enough to make you not go camping anymore—remembering that night on the mountain, bursting out of your tent in a blind panic, but not knowing why, then. And the bed and pillow are drenched with sweat.

I experience feelings of anger and guilt. My concentration and ability to settle has deteriorated to the point where I haven't even read the weekend paper by the time Saturday comes around next. You start to wonder why you can't relax, even for a couple of hours, like guys your own age seem to do, the ones who seem to get through their lives in relative comfort, a tragedy-free and blissfully ignorant life. This brings on feelings of helplessness, of being outside normal society, and difficulties being able to communicate and be "one of the boys," except for those who've been there too. Home, behind the locked doors and windows, and with the barbed wire over the back fence, seems a bloody good option.

I prefer to be at home and not seeing people, more and more. Sometimes I wish it would all just go away. Most people simply don't understand.

With the benefit of assistance through Vietnam Veterans rehabilitation, psychiatric and psychological programs, plus medication, it is obvious that PTSD had a significant effect on how I behaved and tried to manage my life since Vietnam. I am on a veteran's pension and had to stop work a few years ago because of the effects of PTSD.

I only feel an improvement with medication. If I don't take it, life gets difficult. I have tried to change it and get off it, but apparently it's the only solution. Having a wonderful wife—my third—and children and grandchildren are also good things. The best help they can give me is to try to put up with me.

My life and future should be better than it is, but unfortunately the hypervigilance, anger, fear, and other symptoms remain. I think things would be better if we could live away from people, away from the cities and towns.

I Am Learning Not to Take It Personally When He Pushes Me Away

Allison's husband, Sergeant Gilbert, served as a medic in the U.S. Army from 1990 to 2006.

The first time I really noticed a change in my husband was in August of 2005 when he came home on a midtour leave from Iraq. It was his third tour, and the change in him from January until then was really dramatic and frightening in some ways.

He had always been a very affectionate and outgoing person, but on that leave he was very sullen and withdrawn. It was not until after he was diagnosed with PTSD that we both looked back over the last five years and realized that the changes had been happening for a long time, just gradually.

My husband had experienced several traumatic events— being in Iraq so much took a toll. He believes that being on the front lines and in the middle of firefights and then having to treat the wounded right after intensified it. He was also involved in two severe explosions seven days apart on his last tour; those are what finally made him realize that he did indeed need help.

My husband was actually the one who approached the subject first, though after he had gone back, I had done some research online and realized that he probably had PTSD. He had joked about it before, and the changes in him were textbook from what I was able to find. I was afraid to bring it up to him because I didn't want him to think I saw him as "broken." When he got back overseas, he met with a psychologist who has become a huge part of our lives. After he spoke with her, he e-mailed me, and his words broke my heart; at the same time they were giving me hope and confirmation. The psychologist explained to him that his reactions on leave and his behavior were all very normal and that he did have a legitimate problem. He apologized to me for the way he had acted and asked me to help him learn and understand PTSD.

His treatment was started immediately when he got back in January of 2006 and was all his idea. He was very anxious to start healing and learning to cope with his PTSD. I was invited to a few sessions and learned a lot as well. That ended when he left the army in April of 2006 at the end of his last enlistment. They offered a medical discharge for his hearing but not for PTSD. He did not take it, though, because of the amount of time it would have taken to do the paperwork, and he didn't want to extend.

Since then he has been unable to find anyone besides other vets that he feels comfortable talking to, and the VA services for PTSD are still lacking in our area. He gets frustrated now because he is looking and cannot find anyone professional—all of his "therapy" comes from talking to vets in the area and friends.

Being a nurturer by nature, I at first wanted to be right in the middle of his counseling and everything, trying to help and make things better. Unfortunately, that made things worse, and I would get hurt or offended when he pushed me away. Now, I sit back and only offer help when he asks or seeks it. It is hard at times because I hate to see him hurting and wish I could take away the pain, but I am learning that I can't and to not take it personally when he pushes me away. Depending on the situation, he does accept some help from me. If he has a nightmare or a flashback, he will actually seek me out to soothe his nerves and remind him that he is home and safe. Other times, he wants me as far away as possible when he is having a hard time. Other family members are a different story: fortunately, we have a large number of veterans in our family, and their reaction to his diagnosis was very positive. He will talk to them anytime anywhere, while he does not like to talk to me directly about any of his experiences. I learn a lot just by fading into the background and listening, which has helped me to know when to offer help and when to just stand back and let him have his space. The older vets in our family are among our biggest supporters and have made my husband feel better about his diagnosis. He finally realizes he isn't alone, and it doesn't make him "weak" to have PTSD.

Neighbors and friends have been supportive as well, although it takes a lot of discussion and question answering before they get a full understanding of what PTSD is exactly.

My husband is also trying to organize an informal "rap group" in our area, so I have stepped into the administrative role on that, assisting him to organize information, gather resources, mail information, etcetera. These rap meetings are more relaxed than organized therapy—like sitting around rapping or talking with your friends.

The difference between the man I married and the one I live with now is like night and day. When we got married, he was a very outgoing, outspoken, always up for adventure and something new, and an affectionate guy. Now, depending on his mood and what triggers are around, he can be very introverted, sullen, quiet, and he is no longer the type of person who shows affection easily. There are still times when I catch sight of the man I married, and I cherish those times even more; they were taken for granted in the past, and it hurts to think that we have lost that part of our lives. He is slowly regaining that carefree attitude, but it is going to take a while, and I know that it will never be that same way again.

There were two disturbing events that really stand out in my mind. One was about a month after he returned home, and we were still trying to teach our son about triggers and such. My husband was on the computer, and our son walked into the room from behind him. My husband has significant hearing loss due to the two explosions he was involved in, so he didn't hear our son call his name. Without a thought, the child tapped him on the shoulder and startled him—next thing I knew, he had our son pinned on the floor! Only being seven, of course he started to cry and was terrified, which triggered my husband even more. Luckily I was in the room and was able to intervene and talk my husband down before anyone was hurt.

The other incident happened while we were driving on the interstate, going to visit family. We were behind a semitruck, and I noticed smoke coming from its rear tire. Just as I was about to tell my husband the tire was going to blow, it did. My husband had a flashback, tramped the gas pedal to the floor, and almost ran off the road. The whole time he was yelling about RPGs (rocket-propelled grenades) and mortars while I was trying to talk him into pulling over. We finally made it to the side of the road and sat there for about twenty minutes while I talked him down. After he was calm, he couldn't even remember where we were driving to, so I had to take over.

Since his diagnosis things have been slowly changing for the better. At first he wasn't aware of his mood fluctuations, his impatience, or his temper and of their effect on those around him, but now he is, because he has a better understanding of why he feels the way he does. The nightmares and flashbacks are not nearly as common as they were, though that also depends on the time of year and whether he has anniversary dates coming up—when he does, they become more intense and frequent. I see subtle changes in his behavior now about a week in advance of those dates, and he accepts gentle reminders about his moods and temper. His last tour was really rough, and I know which dates may trigger him, so we work together, and at those times we keep things very low key at home so that he has the time and space to work through them.

Generally I look at the calendar and see what types of functions and things we have coming up. I then give my husband the details and let him decide if he thinks he can handle the event, whether it's a school event with our son, a party with friends/family or whatever, and if he says he cannot handle it, I go alone or take our son and attend. Everyone we know is very accepting of this and understands when my husband chooses to stay home.

Our family life has changed to a calmer, more mellow attitude. In some ways PTSD was a blessing in disguise because we all are learning to relax and take a "time-out" when we need to. Before, we were always on the go and running from one event to another. My husband has lost interest in some hobbies but is finding others to take their place: before, his hobbies were always involved with large groups, whereas now he enjoys things he can do alone or with smaller groups. He avoids large gatherings and crowds most of the time and makes sure he can find a quiet place when those cannot be avoided. His social contacts have fallen off, except for close friends from the army.

At times I feel emotionally traumatized more than anything else. When my husband is having a bad spell, I become the "enemy." Though I am learning to not take it personally when he vents or rages at me, it can at times become too much. I know that he loves me, and I have heard him tell other people that he doesn't know how he would survive without me being his rock, but I do sometimes feel neglected and unappreciated. He is nowhere near as affectionate as he used to be, and I think that is the hardest thing for me to deal with—I miss that most of all.

The things that I have found that help me the most with my issues from his PTSD are my online groups that I am a member of and being able to talk to the spouses of the older vets in our family. My mother is also a big support and help because her father was a career air force man and served in World War II, Korea, and Vietnam. So even though she isn't married to a vet with PTSD, she grew up with one, without having a name for it. The other big thing that helps me to cope is really taking the time to take care of myself. I am slowly learning that unless I am taking care of myself, I can't help my husband or our son to cope.

The biggest burden on our family is trying to make our son understand what Dad is going through and allowing him to still be a kid while regulating his behavior when my husband is coping with a particularly bad time. Some days our son isn't even sure how to approach Dad. It is sad to see, but when my husband is really suffering with the moodiness, flashbacks, and other PTSD-related symptoms, our son will avoid asking him even the simplest question for fear of being yelled at or reprimanded. I become the peacekeeper at those times and try to explain to our son that it isn't anything he has done because he sometimes feels that way. When they are so young it is hard to shield them and at the same time educate them so that they understand.

Then there are other days when they are the best of friends like they used to be, and I mourn the loss of that part of our lives all over again, even as the sight of them playing catch melts my heart and puts a smile on my face.

I Attempted Nine Suicides

Pat served in the Canadian army from 1982 to 2007 as a truck driver/operator.

⚬

While deployed to former Yugoslavia, I experienced many traumatizing events: we were not allowed to shoot back unless we were shot at directly, but then it would be too late. We had to face accidents with children, and we had to pick up human bodies to help clean the area so people could return to normal life. I was also being held hostage during a peacekeeping duty—something that you would never think of.

I felt scared and sad, and I felt a lot of rage inside because we were not allowed to do anything. I felt useless out there, as if I was being abused and my hands had handcuffs on.

I've been suffering from PTSD since fall 1998, when I was thirty years old. My wife says that when I came back from my deployment, she noticed that my humor had changed. I started getting very short-fused, and I became scared of being around people, even those that I love. During that time, instead of locking myself in, I got a second job and a third job. I did not have time to think about anything but working, and I had no family life. I went to the doctor for help in January 1999, but I was told that my childhood was the source of my problems. I replied that the nightmare I was going through had nothing to do with my childhood but only with the experiences from former Yugoslavia that were coming back as flashbacks.

I did not know where to go or what to do, and I pushed away my own family. My wife says that my behavior changed completely. I was depressed and attempted nine suicides. Eventually my wife told me that if nothing would be done, she would be leaving with the kids. So after a period of eight years and lots of suffering, I was finally diagnosed with PTSD in January 2006 and medically discharged from the forces in January 2007 due to PTSD and injury.

I'm under psychological and psychiatric treatment. It is very hard for me to control my temper, but with "tools" from the specialist I can manage—not very easily, though, and sometimes I have to bite my tongue so I don't hurt people. I was a very patient man before I got to former Yugoslavia, but on my way back everything frustrated me. My driving has changed quite a bit, and I became a very aggressive driver, especially when people do not respect safety rules. As a transport driver it's, of course, not very good to be like that. My wife says that my mood changes frequently, that I'm prone to verbal abuse, and that my family tries to be gentle when talking to me so I do not lose my temper. She noticed that I changed my attitude towards people—I used to smile and be very social with others. I don't like to be in crowds anymore because I always think that I won't be able to leave the crowded area.

I do not watch anything on TV about wars or people dying senselessly. As soon as people talk about the military or war, I start feeling very lonely. I always feel at fault when something happens at home or in school where I do woodwork. It is a lot harder for me to deal with men when problems occur than with women and to sit down and try to resolve the problem. I believe this is because I was held captive more than once and got hit several times. I get so mixed up that during the night I do round checks inside my house. That's because I got abused every time we went through a checkpoint.

I can hardly sleep at night, even with the pills the doctor gives me. The flashbacks still occur, and so do the nightmares. They've become frequent and have been getting worse even with therapy. The hardest thing is to live with the emotions and accept the situation so that I can improve my living. Now I have sleep apnea, and I need machines that provide pressure during inhalation to be able to breath and sleep properly. My depression is always present, and I need to take medication to be able to live life like others.

I used to hide because I could not take many people around me, and my wife had to explain everything to her family so they'd understand. We lost a lot of friends, but the group at OSISS (Operational Stress Injury Social Support) helps us. My wife accompanies me to my appointments with the psychologist and psychiatrist and helps me by talking to me and trying to understand me. What's very hard for me is my pain inside because I cannot talk and open up to others the way I would love to.

I am now an overly sensitive man, and with everything that happens to my family, I become very aggressive. My wife has to be guided by a specialist who helps us to get through step-by-step. My PTSD has affected her very much: she used to take everything on her shoulders and got burnt out from it. We have a nineteen-year-old daughter and an eighteen-year-old son. Both of them have been affected too but in different ways: Our daughter kept away from home a lot more, and our son was psychologically affected. My family says that accepting and understanding PTSD is a great burden on them; however, they are learning to adapt themselves to the situation.

I have good days and bad days. PTSD is one of the most difficult things to go through, even with the guidance by a specialist. I have been experiencing improvement very slowly. The visits to my psychologist still take place weekly. Medication has helped a lot and finding something that I love to do, either manually or physically. My family has been a huge help—if they would not have supported me, I probably would not be here anymore.

I won't be able to work for anyone for a while—as long as I am not able to take orders from others. So I will construct my own garage and enjoy woodwork inside and being able to choose my own timetable without being pushed. I hope that my flashbacks and nightmares will stop and that I will be able to go through crowded areas again. I hope I will be able to live life normally again.

I Was Certain
I Was Going Crazy

Chief Hospital Corpsman Gordon served in the U.S. Navy from 1979 to 2004. He was an independent duty corpsman, worked in the Fleet Marine Force, and was a surface warrior and career counselor as well.

〜

I joined the navy at the age of twenty-seven—old for a person going into the service—but I was young looking and had a medical background. I was trained for surviving almost any environment by the Marine Corps and navy.

My first traumatic experience occurred during the invasion of Grenada in 1983 in the Caribbean during the Cuban expansion of the area. Watching the injured come to Puerto Rico's Roosevelt Roads Naval Hospital was a little startling: Here were guys our age, coming in all shot up, some even dead in body bags. All I thought was, "Wow, that could have been me fighting with the Marines and SEALS." We spent three days in semilockdown, waiting for the eighty-eight injured and twelve killed in action to be flown in by the Lockheed C-130 Hercules, and sent to the hospital on the medical evacuation bus that I drove. I got to see it all and took it in stride, but holy smoke. . . . I could have been one of these guys. Then three to four days later they were loaded back on my bus and sent to Walter Reed Army Hospital or Bethesda Naval Hospital or wherever there was a bed. None of them looked much better going out; some had more bruising, and others even lost limbs because of loss of blood or too much destruction of tissue that needed to be removed in surgery. I only saw three or four Cuban soldiers come through the hospital. Most was a blur; on a moment's notice we drove to a hanger at the airfield, unloaded twenty stretchers, and went up to the hospital. A quick triage by a doctor or senior corpsman, and we hurried through our maze to get the arrivals registered, screened again, vital signs checked, dressings checked, X-rayed, taken off to a bed or surgery for hours on end, and then it was sit and wait for another call. I don't remember eating or sleeping for three days—just driving, loading, screening, restocking the bus, and going back to the hanger.

There were many more traumatic events:

I experienced a fearful scare when we sailed over a "mine" off Iraq in 1991 during Desert Storm. We were on an ammunition ship with a million pounds of explosives and a million gallons of jet and diesel fuel.

During the conflict in Bosnia-Herzegovina we lived in a gravel pit and walked a mile and a half to our airfield. We also took a convoy of six vehicles to resupply NATO forces, 300 miles a day through Bosnia. There were mines and bunkers with machine gunners waiting for "bad guys," but the question was, who decided who was the bad guy? The trips through Bosnia were scary every day. There were reports of mines planted next to the roads and concertina wire ten feet off the road on both sides. Minefields were everywhere. We worried about being shot at every turn; we worried about being shot up by our allies as we came around the bends of the road. We found three mass graves with our spotter planes and two areas where troops had hidden with large collections of tanks and trucks. Everywhere you looked, every house was shot up by either tank rounds or mortar rounds or bullets. No home was left untouched. The high power lines were cut, and then the towers were blown up to make sure no one could have electricity. All the tunnels were presumed to be booby-trapped with explosives. Farmers were putting mines next to the road to empty their fields, but several of our hummers were still blown up. We had no armor on any of our hummers.

After 9/11, our guided missile cruiser sat off San Francisco. We were standing guard, waiting for any other planes that might have been planning to crash into something—our job would have been to shoot down an American jetliner with our missiles to prevent any further attacks.

During Operation Iraqi Freedom we were sitting fifteen miles off the Iraqi coast near the inlet that went into Umm Qasr. We were well within range of a short-range missile from Iraq or Iran, and I smelled chemicals that resembled nerve agents. I was very concerned because my nephew was ashore during this deployment: he was with a Marine group that guided the Marines to shore for the attack on Baghdad. I did not want to escort his body back to our family and his wife and children—it would have been very painful. He is like a son to me.

Another time, we were chasing drug runners off the Central American coast at night. Not knowing what kind of weapons they had on their boats, and if they were going to spot us and open fire, was unnerving and scary and at the same time exciting.

Going through these experiences took its toll: I started to get very short tempered and to explode very easily. I became verbally abusive, I was having trouble sleeping, and my concentration slipped, which I just explained to my supervisors as fatigue from being up all night for flight operations when I was actually off duty. My appetite dropped off to almost nothing. I spent most of my time drinking coffee and just kept working—or looked like I was working: it is easy to walk around with a blank piece of paper as a supervisor and look important when doing nothing.

I retired from the navy two years ago. Some of my problems started six months after retiring: I had no structure or pattern to follow for my "normal life." I joined some local groups, hoping to find comradeship, only to find myself lost in the shuffle and feeling very alone. I got a job, driving a bus, to make sure people were around me, only to be used as a scapegoat and "gofer" for the company (go for coffee, bread, do the banking, do the building maintenance, find some computers, fix the computers, drive the bus). All this did was make me angry and feel unimportant. Then I would come home and tell my wife my tale of woe, only to hear her say, "Tell them to do more themselves or quit." That was when I started having flashbacks—I was having them while driving down streets. I was also having difficulties sleeping, waking several times after falling asleep late, after midnight. I would go to work grumpy and get mad within the first hour, with ten more hours to go. However, while driving a bus to take seniors shopping or to doctor appointments, it was easy to prevent the office people from seeing me fall apart. I could joke with the passengers to get my mind off the anger and frustration, and I wound up working late and having a fight with my wife about coming home late. Being tired in addition from not having slept well at night, I wanted to destroy anything I could get my hands on.

I started drinking more and enjoying it less: no buzz, no laughter, just apathy. Sex became a joke. I even thought of looking for a girlfriend on the side so I didn't have to listen to my wife complain, but I wouldn't have been able to have sex with her either. I was always too tired to care, even though I wanted attention. I was constantly fighting with my wife: stupid stuff ticked me off, and we would just argue. I would go to work and, if irritated, make an excuse to leave so I didn't have to listen to crap from some of the old ladies that visited the Senior Center where I worked. Yet I acted charming to the old ladies, and they all loved me. Deep inside I hated myself and my way of life. During that time I wrote to my nephew, who is still in the Marine Corps, to watch out for my type of symptoms because he was "up close and more personal" with the waging war in Iraq.

I lost interest in everything: I used to build shelves and little things for the house—I threw away all my wood. I enjoyed playing computer games—I deleted all of them, besides the one I really liked. This one I played for hours late into the night till 2 to 3 A.M., even though I had to get up at 6 or 6.30 A.M.

I met a woman who managed a local apartment complex and whose husband had been with the army in Vietnam. I started seeing her to vent. She listened to me without fighting or judging what was going on in my head. We would talk for hours, and of course my wife found out and assumed I was having an affair, which brought up more fighting and stress.

I kept hearing my kids ask, "What is wrong with Gordy? He is always moody and evasive." My grandson told my wife one day, "Grampa doesn't like people, does he?" If we went out to a party, I would just sit there and drink, ignoring anyone around me—even the people I worked with and some very close friends.

Actually, I was certain I was going crazy. After thinking about just killing myself to stop the misery and pondering how to commit suicide without anyone ever finding me, I decided I couldn't live like this.

I was due for a physical for work and started telling the doctor what was going on. He diagnosed and explained PTSD to me, which I should have figured out, with the twenty-five years in the navy doing a nurse practitioner type of job. I just couldn't fix myself on my own. He prescribed Zoloft and suggested a counselor, and also my wife decided it was time to talk to someone. At that point I had been retired from the navy for about a year and a half. After some counseling the flashbacks waned, and the anger was better under control.

I used to be warm and outgoing—now I just want to be left alone. I gave up all the groups that might have given me camaraderie and stay home and watch TV. To satisfy my wife, I do go out for dinner on Friday but do not enjoy it.

My friends are limited, but the ones that I talk with are very supportive and understand the issues involved.

I still have all of the problems I already had in the beginning, I have a short attention span and am easily distracted during driving trips. I'm having flashbacks of places I was during different conflicts as I do my normal daily activities. When I saw the movie *The Guardian*, I almost ran out of the theater—it is about a coast guard and a swimmer who lost a close friend. I flew on helicopters during the Grenada era and almost died from a crash and lost a friend on a flight I was supposed to be on. The night of the crash I spent seven hours flying around, looking for the wreckage, only to have another plane find it at daybreak. My flashbacks will never fully go away. Depression follows me all the time, and binge drinking happens a lot: I would even drink more, but I need to be sober to drive my van for work. I really have to concentrate or focus on tasks and can almost forget about things if not reminding myself with notes. I have sexual dysfunction, and loss of interest in sex also occurs a lot. I'm still not sleeping well and keep going back and forth between the completely sleepless nights and the late nights, during which I wait to fall asleep. Over-the-counter sleep aids do not help, so I lie there listening to my wife snore and traffic driving by.

If I have been fighting with my wife, the stressors increase the flashbacks and anger toward some poor schmuck that irritates me. I also get very short tempered and aggressively sarcastic in responding to people. I am skilled at cutting people down verbally after spending twenty-five years in the military, telling them to go to hell and convincing them they are going to enjoy the trip. Sometimes again, I am very curt and bitter when speaking to others. Some days, dealing with other people's problems just pisses me off, and I keep thinking, "If you have a problem, see a professional. Stop whining about your life being so screwed up and fix it." I don't interact with too many people because I don't want to listen to their complaining.

At least I saw some improvement in the symptoms of PTSD with the meds, but the daily stressors sometimes negate the effects of the drugs as well as my drinking to try to forget whatever is driving me insane. Zoloft does help with some of the irritability, but the side effects cause more frustration. Counseling and changing jobs to get away from the extreme pressure situations of multitasking also have led to some improvement. Some days are still worse than others. I do all right if I get enough sleep and take my medication, but if I'm tired, I am grumpy and get irritated easily unless I'm preoccupied with caring for the passengers I transport at my new job. I do okay if the weekend "honey-do list" is things I like or want to do, and I do okay if I can get away, but that seldom happens.

My outlook is still bleak. I'm not expecting to ever be normal again. I would like to be happy, but the only way to do that is to get away from my current life and take a giant step backwards: to go back to the area I grew up in and start fresh in a "comfort zone" of old school friends and a slower pace.

One Owns Up to
It Relatively Late

Oberfeldwebel (Staff Sergeant) S. H. has been serving as a soldier in the mountain infantry of the German army since 2000.

I was deployed to Afghanistan in 2004, when I was twenty-four years old. It was already my second deployment—2001/2002 I had been to the Kosovo. On October 6, we came under missile attack in Kabul, Afghanistan: We were on lookout duty, and I was awakened by the firing of three missiles, which flew relatively low over our tanks. Later on in the day, I took part in a search through several caves. In the afternoon we found out that one of the caves that we had entered in the morning had been the launch site for the missiles. Inside the cave was a kind of second cave that could be reached through a small hole in the corner of the larger one and which we had overlooked in the morning. There were five more missiles there, as well as blankets and a fireplace. I still can remember the event relatively well: I can re-play the entire day like a movie in my mind. During the firing of the missiles and everything else that had followed, I didn't think at all. I functioned as if under remote control and acted as I had been trained to.

For me, it was a very drastic experience when the situation with the cave had been clarified. I was swearing and reproach-ing myself for not having seen that the launching place had been inside the cave. Then another staff sergeant put his hand on my shoulder and said I should be glad that nothing had hap-pened. At this moment I realized all of a sudden what we had experienced and survived. I was struck with fear, and I started trembling, breaking out in sweat, and had trouble breathing. It was like a minor breakdown, and it took me five minutes to get myself halfway under control, get my senses together, and start functioning again.

Shortly after my deployment, I started having diarrhea over a longer period of time. In my sleep, I had flashbacks: I was right in the middle of the event. I saw the missiles flying, and everyone was looking at me. I felt like paralyzed, unable to give orders. I screamed in my sleep, and that's when I woke up. In the begin-ning I had these dreams several times; then they stopped. The physical symptoms continued with pounding of the heart, prob-lems breathing, and breaking out in sweat during the night. This all increased further till I started showing physical symptoms whenever I got into unfamiliar situations that I couldn't "con-trol" and if there were a lot of people around, for example, when shopping. That year I didn't go to any discos, not to any place that was unknown to me. Dark rooms turned into a problem too. I tried to avoid such situations at all costs. There was one res-taurant that I was still able to visit, one that we had always gone to. When I was sitting at a place from where I could observe the door, I was able to take it for about an hour. But really comfortable I felt only at home.

I became very irritable, especially in my relationship. On the other hand, I became emotionally numb, and even today, many things sometimes leave me cold: for example, if my girlfriend is almost moved to tears by a television report, I am completely without emotion. It doesn't touch me in the slightest.

When the missiles were fired, it was almost dawning, and as soon as I become aware that it's getting light outside, I'm instantly awake and cannot go back to sleep—independent of what time I went to bed or how I'm feeling. As a rule, I wake up between 5 and 6 o'clock. I've tried all kinds of things to go back to sleep again but haven't had any success so far. If the room is completely dark, however, then I may even sleep until 9 or 9:30.

My symptoms have increased over the years, and some got really severe. I withdrew more and more and broke off my social contacts, until I only stayed home. I greatly reduced my hobbies and had no interest in anything and did nothing anymore. All I wanted was to be left alone, to play my computer games and that nobody would bother me. There was nothing left of my circle of friends outside of the military except for the hard core that I've always had. During that time, my relationship was also suffering because of my continuous excuses as to why I couldn't come along in the evenings. I couldn't very well say that dark rooms made me panic. Then there were always questions like, "Why all these excuses? Have you planned something else?" I've had big fights with my girlfriend, and we almost broke up.

The only thing that I would still leave my apartment for was to ride my mountain bike. Then I could switch off for a few hours—but only with headphones and music in my ears, so that I would blend out as much as possible of my surroundings. I completely concentrated on riding my bike, and that was very restful.

In April 2007, I came home from work one evening, and my apartment smelled of fried liver that my girlfriend had been cooking. In Kabul we once had an incident while I was on guard duty: a small child had been placed outside our gate who had stepped on a mine. We provided first aid and handed it over to a medic. The child had smelled just like the fried liver—like burned flesh. I had been looking forward to a nice evening, but then I completely flipped out, just because of that smell. I went into the cellar and cried for two and a half or three hours. It took me all that time to get a hold of myself and to be able to enter my apartment again. This experience was actually the last building stone in a row that made me admit to myself that I had a serious problem. At first, one wants to disavow it, and one owns up to it relatively late: it was two years after my deployment.

I went to the troop physician and was written sick for two weeks, which did not really help me. During these two weeks I hardly ever left my place. Then I was admitted to the psychiatric department of the military hospital. I stayed there for six weeks in individual therapy with a psychologist and afterwards was treated on an outpatient basis four times within three months. In the beginning, I took thirty milligrams Remergil, which was reduced to fifteen milligrams daily after the six weeks. After three more months, we let it phase out. Now I'm just using it as a sleeping pill on weekends, if I have the feeling that I definitely won't be able to sleep through. Although I'm rarely suffering from sleeping disorders anymore, they still do occur now and then, and this is the symptom that still burdens me most.

I asked to be declared "not suitable for deployment." I'm glad it's no longer possible now that I get sent on a deployment, as are my girlfriend and my parents.

My family and friends were shocked about my diagnosis, even though they had already figured that I may have a problem because of my extreme withdrawal. However, since PTSD is not widely known yet, it didn't tell them much. When I explained to my close friends why I was acting the way I was, why I had outbursts, and what had happened in Afghanistan, they showed nothing but understanding, especially for how I behaved, for example, why I had canceled our evening out four times in a row, despite having agreed at 5 p.m. to go out. Then, at 8 p.m., I canceled, saying that I'm tired and that I would stay at home. Now I can speak openly to my friends or my parents about it. They also confirm that I'm making progress, and that definitely helps me in return.

The first improvements already showed during the six weeks in the military hospital. I felt stabilized and strengthened, and for a beginning, I knew what was wrong with me. There was no noticeable change yet, but I started feeling better. We had numerous conversations about the subject, and bits and pieces of my problem began breaking off inside of me. Now I can pretty much speak about it without getting emotional. Half a year later, the first clear improvements showed. That's when my zest for life returned: I was looking forward to summer a lot, and I really enjoyed it and did many things again that I had not done for the last three years.

To this day I still have to cope with my exaggerated carefulness, though. When I have to leave my apartment, I make precise plans and am careful not to forget anything. I have to write down all the things I need to do outside, like going to the bank, shopping, etcetera, on little scraps of paper to remind myself again while leaving my place. It thus takes me about ten to fifteen minutes before I get out of my apartment.

I am still working on improving my condition. Conversations about deployments with my comrades in the army depress me a lot. Being confronted with news about Afghanistan on television or in the papers is also difficult for me. My body sometimes still reacts to videos and when I'm in cramped places and crowds. However, in my therapy I have learned how to handle these situations: before, I practically fled out of department stores—now, I first observe my surroundings, take a few deep breaths, and then the fear, the physical sensation, and shortness of breath vanish, and I can continue shopping. It still happens, but not so often anymore and mostly in unfamiliar places.

I would say in any case that my confrontation with the trauma has brought something positive for me: I came out strengthened from the situation—nothing much can throw or shock me now. I also know my body and mind better. I am better balanced, the relationship with my girlfriend has strengthened, and we can talk about everything, unlike before. My close circle of friends has become even closer. There is no more contact with the rest, those mere acquaintances, but I'm no longer interested in these people anymore anyhow.

I would advise soldiers suffering from PTSD to get professional help and not to put it off, to inform friends, parents, and other people in one's immediate environment at an early point, so that misunderstandings can be avoided—for outsiders it is not always understandable why one has decided or behaved in a particular way—and to talk about one's experiences, over and over again, no matter with whom. The more I talked about them, the more I was able to distance myself from them, and the physical reactions became less.

PTSD Has Totally Robbed Me of the Man I Married

P. S. is married to a military engineer in the Canadian army. He has been a construction maintenance technician, serving since 1979, and is currently waiting for a medical release due to PTSD and a degenerated disk in his back.

My husband went to Croatia in September 1992 and came back a changed man. He never has and still doesn't let that six months of hell go. He still talks about the events that happened over there:

How, while they were driving, a car coming from the opposite direction would often steer extremely close, playing chicken to see which one would drive into the mined ditches. They lost lots of side mirrors this way. Or the enemy would come from behind and bump into their vehicle, trying to push them into the mined ditches.

He talks of the elderly lady who was being left to die on the side of the road with both legs missing, of the body he saw hanging from a tree, and the horrible sights at a hospital for the mentally handicapped, where the doctors and nurses had left the patients to fend for themselves.

He still sees the young teenager on the sidewalk, pointing an M72 rocket launcher at their vehicle while they were on patrol. My husband reached for his weapon, waiting to see the next move; luckily the young man turned, and my husband could see the barrel was empty. This boy just turned and laughed, not realizing the damage he had done and how close he had come to death.

He remembers the young boy of about nine years who was playing soccer with some other boys and a few of the troops in a field. When the game was over, the little boy ran to his grandfather's tractor to start it. The field was mined and blew him and the tractor to pieces.

My husband has never forgotten that sight.

They sent him back to Macedonia in December 1998, and he lasted one month. He called me every day, crying that he was sick and wanted to get out of there. He told me he was very vigilant and trusted no one. He carried a stick everywhere he went because of the wild dogs and made sure he stayed with other troops because he felt as if the citizens were after him. He developed a groin hernia and what they thought a bronchitis, so they sent him home. When he arrived in Canada, they found he had a bad case of pneumonia.

At that time, I didn't realize what was wrong. I thought he didn't love me anymore. We had always been so affectionate, but he seldom touched me, and it seemed he was always in the next room playing his guitar or listening to music. He never wanted to talk, except about overseas, and then he would get so angry—even today he can't seem to let it go. He was very impatient and hateful to our son.

After twelve years of anguish, flashbacks, nightmares, hyperarousal, anxiety, memory loss, gastrointestinal problems, tremors, and numbing, our daughter, who has a friend with PTSD, said she could see the symptoms in her dad.

My husband was approached by one of his coworkers, who is a nurse. She also spoke to me about his angry outbursts and sent him home a couple of times, as she feared he would strike someone. She suggested I go with him for his next visit to the doctor. I told him what was said between myself and his coworker, and he wholeheartedly agreed for me to accompany him and help him explain everything. My husband always kept these issues and feelings hidden from the doctors. As soon as I talked with his doctor in front of him, she suggested that he be assessed by a psychiatrist. My husband saw the psychiatrist and was diagnosed with PTSD and depression in July 2004. He was also willing to accept help from me and our three children. I know he needs his space and quiet time as well. I now do understand more of what has been happening, and together we can face it.

At the time of his diagnosis, my husband was very emotional and always crying. He had low self-esteem and felt as though no one wanted him around. He felt useless at work, was not sleeping well, had bad nightmares, was not eating and was losing weight. He lived every day as though he were back in Croatia and compared situations at home with the situation there: for example, if the kids said they were bored, he would get into a rage and start screaming how useless they were, and if they were in Croatia, they would have something to complain about.

Now, with the help of medication, he is sleeping better. Sometimes he is still emotional, especially around November 11, our Remembrance Day, or when one of his comrades is killed. Remembrance Day brings back memories of who he has lost because of the war: one uncle spent fifteen years in a veterans' hospital in Montreal, not knowing who he was. He was the only survivor in a cookhouse overseas, and he was diagnosed with shell shock. Another great uncle was in the First World War and died after years of suffering with emphysema problems due to the gases they used at that time. His father's twin brother died of cancer as a result of gases used in the Second World War. His dad committed suicide at the age of fifty-eight: he had been treated for years for shell shock, and at the end he still thought the enemy was after him. As for now, my husband has lost comrades to suicide and some to cancer, and whenever there is news of a Canadian soldier killed overseas, he takes each and every one of them very personally, and it hurts him very much.

He still relates a lot to what happened in Croatia, and he also gets very upset if the car behind him gets too close. When we were driving down the street in June 2004, the car in front stopped to let an elderly gentleman out. My husband started screaming and cursing at this old man because he had held up traffic. I couldn't believe it—he always has had the greatest respect and patience with older people. He turned around and drove right back home. He was so frustrated, he sat down and cried for over an hour. Another time, when they brought a dead soldier home, he got so emotional that his CO had to take him to the hospital to see the psychiatrist. They called me at home; I went in and tried to help calm him down. The psychiatrist sent him home for three weeks.

My husband can't watch if there is anything on TV that has to do with war or killing; even the news upsets him. Any program on sexual abuse of women or children he cannot watch because it gives him nightmares. He has difficulties with swallowing due to gastrointestinal problems, so if he gets upset, he chokes when he tries to eat. Even though he is on medication, he is still depressed, full of anger, has very short temper, and no patience. He is hypervigilant, suffering from terrible anxiety, has bad memory loss, shows little affection, and is always full of aches and pains.

Our family life has changed drastically. I find the greatest burden is his not wanting to go anywhere, except to work or to the doctor. If I do persuade him to go on visits or outings, we always end up coming back early because he gets a headache, or nausea, or diarrhea. We used to go every weekend for drives in the country, but we no longer do that. He is so paranoid of the car behind him that he is not comfortable driving. His family lives in the same town as my family: I go home two to three times a year. Usually I can't persuade him to go home even once a year. When the kids come to visit, he doesn't want to go out to dinner or anyplace else. He screams at our oldest grandson if he makes too much noise or complains. He has totally lost interest in keeping up with social contacts, one reason being that he is hypervigilant and trusts no one. His memory is so bad it is hard for him to keep up a conversation—most of the time when talking to me, he forgets what he was talking about. Seeing him trying to remember things in a conversation is so sad. As far as hobbies, he was a great sportsman, cross-country skier, did running, weight training, played hockey, baseball, soccer, broomball, and went bowling. He does none of that now.

It tears my heart out to see my husband cry, to listen to him, and see him hurt so deep inside. I really miss our romantic times, going for walks, drives, and romantic dinners.

I feel that PTSD has totally robbed me of the man I so lovingly married thirty-two years ago.

We have three children: the oldest is in the military. His father's PTSD has not affected him, except that he is very concerned about him. Our daughter has married a military man. She was out and about so much, she didn't seem affected, although once she married and met one of her husband's friends, who has PTSD, she mentioned to me right away that she thought that was what her father had. Our youngest son took the brunt. Not knowing what was wrong with his dad, he thought his dad didn't love him because he was always screaming and cursing at him. Our son got into a little trouble and had to take anger management courses. The course did help him, but he is still more emotional than my other two.

Our children are very understanding now that they know their father has PTSD. They have learned his different issues and have made a point of reading up on PTSD. Although the two boys live in another province, they call weekly to see how he is doing. Our daughter lives close, so she talks to us every day. She has three sons, and when they come over, they know Grampy gets a little tired, and so he goes in another room and plays his guitar.

As far as relatives, I have mentioned PTSD to them, but they don't seem to want to understand it. Our friends and neighbors don't come around much anymore, and my husband doesn't want them to know his problem.

As for myself, my husband's psychiatrist suggested I see someone to help me understand what was happening. I went to a counselor for about eight weeks, and my medical doctor put me on antidepressants, which have a good effect. I am also a volunteer for VAC (Veterans Affairs Canada), helping others cope with their spouses' PTSD.

I Feel Guilty for Everything

Sergeant Dave served two years active duty in the U.S. Army from 1968 to 1970, his specialization being light weapons, infantry. He received Bronze and Silver stars.

At twenty-three, I entered Vietnam. I was assigned the point position (first man in the column) after my first two weeks in country. I walked point about every third day for nearly ten months. It was like playing Russian roulette: my chances of being killed or wounded were about one out of every six missions. Walking point was a traumatic experience every time. I saw five other point men get killed or wounded during my ten months in the jungle.

Walking point required my absolute, complete attention. I let fear peak my adrenaline. My reactions had to be instantaneous. A moment's hesitation could take my life as well as that of those behind me. There could be no distractions, so I quickly learned to shut down my emotions to focus entirely on my immediate surroundings.

After a month and a half, I walked our company into an ambush. My entire squad was killed, and 50 percent of our company was flown back to the hospital. During the ambush, I was almost paralyzed with fear. I thought I'd be killed, and there was nothing I could do about it. I didn't run back to the protection of a large termite mound like the rest of my squad. I thought in those few seconds that it was the dumbest decision I had ever made. I was in shock for several minutes after the big explosion that killed them all. It slowly sank in that the termite mound had been booby-trapped; I felt like someone had kicked me in the stomach. The loss of everyone I knew was overwhelming. I couldn't feel the depths of it—it was too big to comprehend. I wanted to wail in grief but could only force myself to cry a little about half an hour later. I stayed awake all that night reviewing what had happened: Was there something I could or should have done differently? Why or how did I survive? What would it be like with everyone gone? I was the only one left who had lived with them every day; I was the only one who could keep their memories alive.

Four months into my deployment, I was in the hospital with a foot infection. My squad was flown into the hospital: They'd been ambushed again: two dead, the rest wounded.

There were many other traumatizing incidents:

I shot it out with a Vietcong in a foxhole only three feet away. I killed two Vietcong while looking them in the eyes before I pulled the trigger. My rifle jammed while a Vietcong was shooting on full automatic at the guy next to me, and I would be his next target. I saw a Vietcong through ten feet of bamboo, sneaking up behind us; we killed him. I was given a vision of Vietcong coming down a trail we were not watching, an hour before it happened.

In a firefight, time would slow down. Quite often things would seem to be happening in slow motion. I could think out several consecutive thoughts in a fraction of a second. After the firefight was over, my knees would turn to rubber, and I'd have to sit down until the adrenaline subsided. Piecing together what happened often brought out the fear of realizing how things could have so easily gotten worse.

I almost had a nervous breakdown at ten months in the jungle: I couldn't resolve the conflict of protecting those around me by walking point and wanting to survive my last two months so I could go home.

Soon after returning home, I had decided to bury all memories of Vietnam and deny they bothered me. Denial was so strong that all the difficulties in my family had to be related to something or someone else—I was okay. If I admitted Vietnam memories bothered me, then I'd be obligated to deal with them. I wasn't ready to do that for thirty years.

While in Vietnam, I had made up my mind to get into aeronautical engineering when I got home. That dream got buried with everything else about Vietnam. I returned to college after Vietnam, majoring in civil engineering instead, and was offered an exchange with someone in Cambridge to finish my degree, but I couldn't allow myself to leave home again to do that. Memories of Vietnam were always bigger than my job. I couldn't dedicate myself completely to any career.

My anger started flashing easily. Still today, I experience instant anger at the perception of what I might consider injustice or arrogance. Road rage is another of my problems, as well as anxiety. There were intrusive thoughts, flashbacks, and problems sleeping. I felt different from the rest of society and couldn't talk about what had happened. I isolated myself from everyone and still do so today. I am less confident around people. My self-image is poor because people didn't want to hear about the biggest events in my life—so I felt unimportant and that my experiences and therefore me were worthless. I've felt disillusioned with our society and humanity in general, so I'm probably seen as being more cynical than "normal" people. I don't trust people to do what they profess; I know they can easily change their minds, depending on the circumstances. Relationships became difficult to maintain and still are. I'd much rather avoid people and situations where interaction is expected. I was and still am emotionally numb. My wife and son thought I hated them because I didn't provide any emotional support. I rarely express what's on my heart, even if I could; it would start sounding like a broken record. I still don't catch the emotional cues for appropriate reactions and support of my wife. I have no friends I call close, compared to those in Vietnam. I've lost desire for any recreational activities.

I've been suffering from long-term depression and survivor's guilt. I am self-conscious and take on disproportionate amounts of guilt. I feel guilty for everything. I feel embarrassment from inappropriate reactions. I am depressed about being unable to cope like others.

I've been stuck in survival mode for most of my life. I can't think of anything that is not influenced by PTSD.

I wasn't diagnosed with PTSD until thirty years later. The onset of type 2 diabetes led me into the VA medical system where I learned about PTSD. My life was falling apart at the same time. The only thing I hadn't tried was walking out on my family. There was so much psychological pain that walking away or suicide seemed the only alternatives left. I had tried everything I could think of and nothing worked. At that point, I had to admit I couldn't fix things on my own. Since I was already going to the VA for diabetes, I thought I might as well see if PTSD might be causing some of our problems. I ended up at our local Vet Center for individual and group counseling and underwent cognitive-behavioral therapy for six years. Angry outbursts had become so painful to my wife and myself that we really have tried to limit those times in the last seven or eight years.

Therapy, medication, and support from my family have led to some improvement. The best support one can give me is helping me not to feel so guilty for being changed and unable to get on track with the rest of society.

The single biggest change happened when I accepted that I was not the one in control of what happened in Vietnam and the one who was in control wants what is best for me. Life is not about an event, but rather a process of changes. Nothing will be wasted, and everything can be turned into something good. There is a reality bigger than the limited focus of our culture, including the horrors of our human nature. There are answers that make sense out of all our experiences. Vietnam made me search for those answers like nothing else could have.

Now, thirty-nine years later, I no longer deny Vietnam bothered me. I'm not as confused as I used to be about why I'm so different from normal people. There are important lessons to be learned from Vietnam—it wasn't totally worthless. My anger has subsided somewhat. I still struggle with everything else. I take medication to sleep, for depression, anxiety, and diabetes. Other than that, I'm okay.

Looking back with regret only makes us stumble. We can't see into the future, but we can have a relationship with the one who does see without time.

For Me, the War Is Still On

Stabsunteroffizier (Staff Sergeant) Christian served from 1997 to 2005 in the artillery of the German army.

I was twenty-six years old when I was deployed to Kuwait in March 2003, twenty-four hours after the initial attack on Iraq. I was stationed at Camp Doha, the logistic headquarters of the Americans. It was the first week of combat operations, and we were under massive permanent attack: the Iraqis fired away everything they had, also their Scud missiles. Every time the sirens went off, we had to try to run to a bunker within seconds. That went on for five days, during which we had about thirty alerts day and night. No missiles hit the camp, and I also didn't see any wounded or dead. This permanent enormous stress, the constant danger, however, caused my PTSD. What is still in my body is the drill-like behavior after the alert.

The first few moments, one was concentrating fully on putting on the NBC protective gear as quickly and airily as possible. Afterwards, in the shelter, one sat and waited for what was going to happen. In my diary that I kept there, I found that I was constantly asking myself if the mask was tight, but I didn't remember this, I just read it later. Other than that, I didn't think or feel anything. I concentrated hard on breathing calmly under the mask, which wasn't quite that easy under the hot weather conditions. One was just at the mercy of it all.

After the deployment it took me about a year till I realized that something was wrong with me. However, I already had several symptoms before. Other people can recount this better than I, though: I had been in a relationship for seven years before my deployment and had been living with my girlfriend. About four months after coming back, I separated from her. However, I didn't give any explanation, I just said, "Finished, it's over, I'm going." When my ex-girlfriend talks about it now, she says that she had right away noticed a change in me: I was very easily irritated, everything was too much for me, and I wanted to have my peace. Only I myself didn't notice it.

Then, one morning, when I was getting ready to leave for work, I had an attack—at least, that's what I call it: I felt extremely restless, my heart started pounding, and I was crawling on all fours through my apartment, looking for something—what, I had no idea of. That was the first time I thought that something was wrong. I didn't recognize myself anymore, I had never been like that before. What exactly was wrong with me, I didn't know, however.

I went to the troop physician, told him about the attack, and said that I had no idea where this behavior had come from. On his questioning, I told him that I had been deployed, that I had broken up with my girlfriend, but that I had been able to cope well with everything and had gotten over it. Suspecting stress disorder, he referred me to the military hospital, where I spoke to a psychiatrist three or four times. His rash diagnosis was depression and that I needed conversational therapy. I was advised to look for a civilian therapist because there was nobody available at the military hospital at that time. So, in summer 2004, about one and a half years after Kuwait, a civilian therapist diagnosed me with PTSD resulting from my deployment, and I started therapy. However, we didn't work on my traumatic experiences since we didn't have a chance: things were going downhill so rapidly with me that my therapist had both hands full, trying to help me to at least function somewhat in daily life.

When the first symptoms appeared, I withdrew completely. I locked myself in my apartment for weeks and didn't open any mail, didn't answer the telephone, and didn't open the door. On the other hand, I was constantly trying to meet women, which ended in a catastrophe every time. So, my therapist and I were always busy working through the current problems and situations.

At first, I also had great difficulties driving a car and could just barely do it. It was so strenuous, probably because I was observing the sky more than the road in order to see whether the airspace was clear. Once I passed a truck on the highway which was loaded with gas cylinders. Suddenly, I saw the scenario of a bomb attack before my eyes, and I was "driving into the bomb." I don't know where that came from. When I'm having flash-backs, I'm often experiencing the "incident" so intensively that I don't have images before my eyes—that's what it seems like to me, at least. I usually reexperience the running for shelter, the hectic rush when we had to put on the protective gear and run to the bunker. This is why I'm afraid to exercise because if I'm jogging, for example, I quickly get into a situation where I'm a soldier again, and the tension mounts as it was during missions.

I also was suffering from tremendous headaches, but meanwhile they don't come anymore.

I was medically discharged in December 2004 for depression. For the time after the service, I had planned to train as a professional fireman and had already completed the first courses of rescue medical training while on active duty. But this goal is no longer attainable for me because of my PTSD.

About half a year ago, I was an inpatient in a hospital for thirteen weeks and had trauma therapy for the first time. That was about four years after Kuwait. Their medical reports state that my PTSD was exclusively caused by the deployment, in particular by the heavy one-week attack by Iraqi Scud missiles, and that I developed a recurrent depression from that. I had "thousands" of symptoms, and it took them quite a long time just to stabilize me. What I had and still have the most problems with are helicopter and plane noises or something that sounds like a siren. Sometimes it's also a sound like the starting of a lawn mower, and then my body "thinks" this is the siren, and it's a matter of life and death now. Meanwhile, I'm constantly sounding out if there is danger or not. I don't like being outside of my apartment by myself—if I am, then often with music in my ears to choke out these type of noises, for one frequently hears planes or helicopters.

My worldview has also changed. The deployment, in some ways, went against my personal moral convictions: 4,000 dead soldiers—some of whom I had been eating with, talked with, and I don't know who of them is dead and who is still alive; over 100,000 dead civilians. . . . That's probably where my depression comes from. This is also the reason why I can't cope if I still see the war in Iraq on television.

If I compare how things were before my stay in the hospital and how they have been afterwards, a lot has changed. I was put on medication there for the first time and had many individual and also group sessions. We did EMDR (eye movement desensitization and reprocessing) and worked with the observer method. It was very interesting to see how my body reacts to it: my physical reactions during therapy completely matched what I recounted. My PTSD has not disappeared, however. I still react to certain noises, but what's a lot better now is that my body no longer "starts up." This physical "start-up" is difficult to explain, but it feels as if you were in a situation that's a matter of life or death. I know that I could jump through a window pane then. Before, it was always extreme how my body was pumping adrenaline without end in such situations, and this is now more subdued due to the help of psychotherapy and medication.

I'm still suffering from flashbacks. I've had difficulties breathing a few times in the past, but they don't happen too often anymore: for example, in the hospital I fell asleep one afternoon, woke up, and tried to tear a mask off my face. I was extremely short of breath, as if I hadn't gotten any air at all.

I don't have nightmares, but I can't sleep very well and have lots of difficulties falling asleep. I don't know when this started, but I've had these problems for quite a long time. In the beginning, the tablets helped since they are also sleep inducing, but meanwhile my body has gotten used to them. Last night, at 3:30, there was a fire somewhere, and I was woken up by the fire sirens, fire trucks, and police cars. The volunteer fire brigade was called as well and the school siren was turned on. I briefly started up physically, but then I was quite calm. But somehow it felt as if something were "running along" in the background, which I couldn't shake off, and I couldn't go back to sleep again anymore. I was wide awake.

These are my biggest problems. Ultimately, a lot has gotten better since I meanwhile have a very good understanding of the symptoms. I'm also still working with my civilian therapist.

What's still difficult for me is my exaggerated irritability. My therapist explained to me that the physical symptoms are like a drug for me: my body wants to have this drug, this kick, again and again. At times, when everything was calm, I could barely feel myself, and this tranquillity bothered me so much that I created a situation for myself where I would get emotionally worked up. That happened a lot in relationships: for example, I would "collect" a hundred unimportant little things, petty little matters, and make a mountain out of a molehill to artificially create some action. In combination with my exaggerated irritability this was catastrophic. I always get very sad when I think back how many people I have hurt during the past three years. That was pretty harsh. Meanwhile, it at least has gotten a little better, and I try to build on that.

What also bothers me a lot is that I'm often emotionally numb. Sometimes, I can feel normally, and other times I feel nothing. If I then take my girlfriend into my arms, it feels like holding a dead piece of meat. There were many such situations in the past.

It's been four and a half years since my deployment, but for me, the war is still on. It is very problematic for me that, although I've been back from my deployment for a long time now and am still suffering from the effects, one is still confronted with the war on a daily basis: on TV, the radio, and in the newspapers. It isn't easy to get away from it. On the one hand, I know that it isn't good for me to be too close to it, but on the other hand, I'm still drawn to it. When I'm confronted with the war, I get hung up in it and have difficulties staying in the normal world. I look at videos from the war in Iraq and am no longer here but in the war. I can't really cope with the world here anymore then. When I see how some people in the supermarket fight to be first at the cash register, I cannot understand that at all. Once I really screamed.

When I'm sitting at my kitchen table under the skylight in the morning, I usually am able to evade five or six noises and can somehow distract myself. But at some point, the fifth, sixth, or seventh noise enters my body. I cannot keep it out; it just gets in—that's how I always describe it. Before my stay in the hospital, the situation got so dramatic that I was just sitting there, staring out of the window, watching the "airspace" and smoking one cigarette after another. I was stuck in this state for three to five hours and was completely worn out afterwards. Then I had to lie down and sleep, and after that I was better again.

Fortunately, I don't have a drinking problem, but when I went out once in a while, I tried very hard to push my problems away with alcohol, especially when I was in a disco or a club with many lights, loud music, and people that were enjoying themselves and dancing. I always have extreme problems in situations like these; I can't understand the world any longer then. I'm standing there, with different images, different thoughts, different things on my mind, instead of being cheerful because I have gotten to know a very different world, and it is always present in the background. People often ask me why I hold myself responsible for the war in Iraq. But that's a different story. What I see are these 100,000 dead people from the war, where I was once part of a machinery. That's simply a different world.

I find it hard to keep the war and this world apart, but meanwhile it has gotten a bit better.

Before my deployment, I used to be very active in sports and belonged to several organizations—the soccer club, track and field athletics—and now I don't do any sports at all anymore. Financially, things are not looking good either. I spend a lot of money sometimes, just like that. When I'm on the go and mentally in my other world, I think, "Okay, now look around what other people are up to. They are running about, buying things.

Why don't you do that too?" Then I buy all sorts of things at random that I don't need at all and automatically get into financial trouble. Meanwhile I have that better under control, but for a while it was really bad: I couldn't have cared less if all kinds of bills arrived. I could have received a letter, saying to pay 100 Euro by tomorrow, or I would go to jail, and that wouldn't have bothered me in the slightest.

In everyday life I only did those things that were necessary for survival. I had no regular meals anymore. My PTSD had crawled into everything.

My circle of friends shrank quite a bit—there are two or three people whom I can rely on, who take me as I am, and the rest doesn't exist anymore. My family doesn't understand anyhow, the only exception being my grandparents, who have experienced war themselves.

My therapist at the hospital once asked me why I talk of my trauma as if hardly anything had happened. I said, "Because actually nothing has happened." This is a very stupid idea, but I would have preferred to come home without an arm or a leg, for this everyone could have seen and understood. People, however, do not understand what PTSD is, and I don't hold it against them.

As a beginning, it would be helpful if others showed understanding that when I am not doing well, I don't like to talk on the telephone or call anyone. Many people don't understand this. Till now, no one from my family or friends has said, "Come, let's sit down, and you tell us what kind of symptoms you have." Probably it's because they don't know what they should be asking, and so they leave it at that. I really would have appreciated it if someone would have been interested. But in the end, everyone is fighting his own battle.

I get a lot of encouragement from my current girlfriend, and this helps me a lot. We met in the hospital, and from there, she has some knowledge of the symptoms. She is the only human being I can stand being close to, by now even all of the time. Because of her, I can see many things again that make life in society well worth living. That's why I have hope that things are going uphill because I am able to handle the problem of closeness and distance relatively well with her. What I want on the one hand, what I need, is closeness, also physical closeness—that one takes me into one's arms and holds me. As it very often was the case before, a second later, I couldn't stand that closeness at all anymore. To regulate this was always very difficult, and my emotionless phases are still causing me troubles.

I used to really enjoy life. I never was a great thinker but always did, on the spur of the moment, what I felt like doing. Meanwhile, I'm always thinking and rethinking everything and have lost my easygoing ways. To some degree, I'm also a lot more aggressive than I used to be. I can't allow myself to think about these things because they really drag me down. I hope someday it will get better and be normal again. I find I am a different person. I would say, there is Christian I, there is Christian II, and I hope that soon there will be Christian III and no longer I and II and that everything will be good then, so to speak.

Recently, I have found out that I am not the only one from my deployment that has developed PTSD. Alone knowing that gave me back a lot of my feeling of self-worth, for there were times when I had questioned myself, whether I was imagining things or whether I was mentally unstable.

As for my future, I hope to be able to keep my relationship. Concerning my profession, I'm soon going to start on a new road with the help of the organization Skarabäus: I'll fly to a different city and orient myself completely new. I hope I'll find a job I'd like to do and get going. I used to be very attached to where I grew up—this is gone, nothing holds me back; that's all burned soil for me. So, I'll just go somewhere else and start all over again.

Nothing Will
Ever Be the Same

Jamal is a veteran of Desert Storm, Desert Shield, and Operation Iraqi Freedom. He served since 1981 and retired from the U.S. Army as a sergeant in 2004. Jamal was a heavy military transportation truck driver and an Arabic translator assistant.

The event that caused my PTSD occurred during my deployment to Iraq when I was forty-one years old: We ran over IEDs, and they killed a number of soldiers in front of us in another vehicle. All I remember is that I was very sad and then angered. We captured the guys who did it and were pretty mad and upset.

I was diagnosed with combat stress by the army when I left Iraq. I had enough years in the service, and so I got out. I just didn't want to be there anymore; I didn't want to be on another tour in Iraq. I was a reservist, and when I came back from Iraq, I quit my other job after getting out of the military. I was a prison guard, but that didn't work anymore because of my lack of patience since I returned. I couldn't take the stress. I had trouble finding a new job, but then I got one with a different company and currently work for one of the railroads.

I lost interest in just about everything and in all my hobbies. My marriage fell apart when I came back, and my wife divorced me. She said I was too distant for her and that sometimes I just seemed mean. I have changed a lot. I *am* meaner, a lot meaner—cut-and-dried, that's basically how I am. Lacking emotion is the worst aspect of PTSD for me, that's what I always say. I don't know how to explain it; you have to experience it to understand it. When it comes to combat, you are lacking emotion, you feel distant. I guess you could call it aloof; that's how I sometimes feel—and, I hate to admit, sometimes absolutely ruthless, like a businessman in a big company. I can't stand a lack of confidence in people: if they can't make up their minds, I get irritated and angered easily. I think that's because when you are in the military and in a combat zone, you can't be around people that can't make decisions because you can get killed. I think that went from there to here, in my everyday life.

Every now and then I see something that reminds me of Iraq, and it makes me feel like I'm back. For example, date palms and palm trees remind me of the groves of the Euphrates River. Sometimes, when I watch TV and see Iraq, I know the different cities, and it brings back memories. I don't like to watch programs about the war. I feel it makes things worse for me, so I try to avoid all that, any association with Iraq. I get really mad when people bother me about Iraq. As for the symptoms, I haven't noticed a change over the course of time. I haven't noticed anything worse nor anything better. I avoid talking about it as much as I can; that seems to help. I have one sister, and she is okay when I talk to her. She's pretty cool about things. She listens to some of my stories, and she helps in this way. But I don't like talking much about Iraq; I really don't say much about anything.

My girlfriend says that one day, when she woke me up, I put my hand around her neck. I don't remember that. It scared me, but hopefully it won't happen again. Whenever she wakes me up now, she just tugs my foot. I sort of jump up. She says, sometimes she'll hear me talk in my sleep as if I were in Iraq.

I drink heavily at times but have no other disorders. Every now and then I get a little depressed, and sometimes there is a tightness in my throat. Before, I didn't realize that it is part of PTSD.

I don't have any problems talking with strangers, but I find myself wanting to hang around a lot more with veterans though. Almost everybody I know is getting into the military or is related to the military.

The Veterans Administration gives me medication, and it helps me. I am not as mean; I guess you could say that I am more timid now. I better understand what other people are saying to me instead of just feeling that they are really getting on my nerves. The medication helps you think a little better.

As for my future, nothing will ever be the same as it was before. Everything is different now. I wish my PTSD would go away again, but I don't think it will. There will always be something there. But I got a really good girlfriend that helps me and wants to get married. Maybe things won't be so bad. I'm hoping.

I'm Looking Forward to My Future

Vince joined the Seaforth Highlanders, a reserve infantry regiment of the Canadian army, in 1989. He was deployed to Norway and Croatia, was an instructor with the Princess Patricia's Canadian Light Infantry, and then was a company quartermaster sergeant with the Seaforth Highlanders. He was medically discharged in 2004.

I was twenty-one years old when I was deployed to Croatia in 1993. My patrol was held up and detained by a number of Serbian militia soldiers for almost a full day in a village called Ragoli. We experienced a whole range of feelings:

In the beginning, I felt very fearful and apprehensive; I remember my hands were shaking. Everything seemed very surreal, for some things were moving in slow motion, and I almost felt as if I were watching and seeing my body react and move—yet not watching my body from the outside but watching through my eyes. It calmed down to where things became more normalized, and then at one point, there was an incident: we were trying to get some guys off the vehicle, and we were very angry and aggressive towards them. When everything was over, I felt euphoria that we had survived something like that and were okay, but once that had worn off and we had gotten back to our base, the shakes kicked in again.

In the weeks that followed, I developed all kinds of symptoms: numbing to the world, grudges, controlling behavior; I felt angry, had eruptions of rage, yelled at the TV. At the time, the news coverage was very anti-Serb and Sarajevo focused, and from my point of view, they weren't reporting very fairly. I also had intrusive recall, insomnia, suffered from hypervigilance, and engaged in alcohol abuse. As for the elevated startle response, I'm not sure because in the environment that we were in, those kinds of reactions were actually appropriate. This behavior certainly followed us afterwards.

It was not long after I came back home that there was a fire down the street where a house burned down. The smell triggered me and gave me a bit of a flashback. But I've had very few since; within a short period of time, I've been able to put a finger on and identify that I have been triggered. There are certain things that trigger me that I avoid going to. There is a—sounds silly—produce store that's very narrow and stocked really high with lots of boxes. For some reason—maybe it's like a bunker—it triggers me. When I go in there, I start feeling anxious like at the beginning of an anxiety attack, and I leave. I just can't go into the store.

Agoraphobia is a big issue too. When I go Christmas shopping or if I have to go to the mall, I'll do it first thing in the morning on a weekday, so there are only very few people there. I get out of there before it gets busy, as quickly as I can. Same thing with grocery stores and public events, like the fireworks here in Vancouver, where there are really very large groups of people and close confines: I stay away, if I can, because they are triggering; I don't feel safe.

When I drive, I'll do everything I can to avoid congestion or traffic patterns that I don't feel comfortable with. It drives my wife crazy. I will go by the path of least resistance at all times—even if that means going several kilometers out of my way just to go around something.

I don't put an extra effort into looking for things that trigger me, but I certainly do avoid things.

Intrusive recall is more common for me than flashbacks: I find myself with the "movie" in my head, with the story or sequence just keeping on playing and playing and playing, and it just won't go away.

As for physical outbursts, I have never come to blows with anyone, but I have certainly intimidated people.

For the first five, six years after coming back from our tour with PTSD, I was an alcoholic, drank way too much. That definitely affected my personal life a lot—not being able to have a relationship and being completely dysfunctional. Professionally, I would take a job and do it well for a short period of time, and then I'd become bored or too smart for my own good—smarter than the boss, smarter than whoever—and they would decide that I shouldn't be there anymore. Usually I was pretty good about catching it, being aware that I was going to get fired or moved along, and more often, I quit before they fired me. At that stage, there was no way that I could have successfully attended and completed university or college: I just wouldn't have been able to get my head around to stay focused for an extended period of time.

Before I had PTSD, I would work or attend school, come home, and then continue with normal evening activities, socialize, play sports, baseball, hockey, whatever. Afterwards—before I was diagnosed—I would function at work, go home, and then it wouldn't be uncommon for me to do what I call "locking myself in the basement": if the phone would ring, to simply look at it and let the answering machine get it or just simply turn the ringer right off the phone, to stop talking to friends or family members for months or some people even for years. That period wasn't a good time.

I certainly had no interest in meeting or talking to any non-military friends or people outside of the military. At social events I could be polite, but that would be it; there would be no contact afterwards. I was definitely different from how I was before suffering from PTSD.

I have a hard time trusting people who I feel haven't had similar or the same experiences, with few exceptions. In my opinion, that goes for a lot of people; their priorities in life are completely messed up and not on the important things that I consider worth living for. But I absolutely trust the people that I served with and whom I'm still in contact with.

About eight years after the tour, I had figured that I probably had some issues that I needed to work on, so I did some group work with other soldiers. It wasn't until about two years later that I saw a presentation from a Vietnam veteran who talked about his experiences with PTSD. What I had been doing or going through was remarkably similar. So I picked up a fact sheet on PTSD. I was pretty confident that I'd hit most of the criteria. I handed my wife this sheet, gave her a red pen, and asked her to make a mark by all the things that she sees in me. She handed me back a piece of paper that was covered with red ink. At that point, I said, "Okay, it's time for me to go in and see if there's a diagnosis there." So it was probably ten years after the fact that I sought help and was officially diagnosed. I was out of the military at that time since I had been diagnosed with type 1 diabetes and released from the service with diabetes.

Why did I wait so long? Probably because I wasn't aware that I was injured with PTSD. Up to that point I had thought my behavior and problems were normal and didn't realize that they were not. After I got diagnosed, I started seeing somebody regularly for therapy.

PTSD is a thousand-pound gorilla that's on your back. It affects everything. Fourteen years have passed since the traumatizing event:

I'm certainly hypervigilant and always very aware of my environment. Sometimes I feel anxiety, depending where I am. I also experience grips of controlling behavior; my best example for it is being a terrible backseat driver for my wife, telling her how to drive. As for driving myself, I know the area where I live and work in the city well enough that I can work with that. Interacting with strangers sometimes is difficult for me, also war-related news on TV; I don't watch it most of the time, I just turn it off.

I'm numb, what they call psychic numbing, not to my immediate family, not to my wife and my child, but to the rest of the general world.

I have good days and bad days. On good days, I can be almost symptom free. If I have a bad day and something has set me off or triggered me, then I can definitely experience depression. Memory loss is a big issue for me—it's an indicator that I'm heading down a road where things aren't going very well. When I'm in a downfall, I lose my temper a lot more often, and I experience insomnia—I don't sleep at all or have problems sleeping.

The hardest thing is keeping a grip on PTSD, keeping aware of it, and staying on top of my self-care because the most important thing, the most important people in my life, are my wife and my son, who is seventeen months old. I got to keep that relationship happy and healthy, so I have to keep myself healthy to keep our relationship healthy. I think that's the biggest challenge right there.

I've been seeing somebody for three years—at first it was a psychologist, and now it's a psychiatrist. I did cognitive-behavioral therapy, individual and group cognitive therapy, and with the group therapy, I've also done some reenactment. I don't take medication.

The therapists don't have any magical answers or magic pills; usually, they just help you find the answers that are already sort of buried in your head. They're a neutral sounding board. They are not a family member and thus not influenced by that perspective; they don't judge—they are like supportive friends that are extremely helpful.

I don't have so much intrusive recall now, nor flashbacks. I don't drink like I used to—I drink socially, occasionally, which is less than once a month—and I am much more aware of the onset of my symptoms, of the depression, the insomnia, the memory loss, the concentration problems. I'm more apt to phone my therapist and say, "Okay it's time to go in and check this out."

My wife is very aware of my symptoms as well. Usually, she catches me before I do: we have an agreement or understanding that if I start going down and showing symptoms, she'll tell me flat out to go see the psychiatrist. As well for myself, if I find myself starting to get short of temper, starting to not sleep very well, then it's time for me to see my psychiatrist. We try to catch it before it's a serious problem because when I'm not doing well, I start affecting her, and then our communication goes downhill, and we start fighting. And then it just doesn't turn into a happy home.

The kind of support I get from my family, also from my parents, is that they are simply being empathetic, not sympathetic, and have an understanding of some of the symptoms and things that affect me. I know with my close friends and my family that if I needed just somebody to talk to and be with, I could pick up the phone, and they would be there. If I needed to meet somewhere to talk, to go and have a coffee with, or to go grab a sandwich with, they would do that as well. This is how my friends who have PTSD and I support each other. They're empathetic, they're honest, and sometimes it hurts. But being brutally honest helps. A friend will give you a kick in the ass, and sometimes you need that.

To support someone with PTSD, people don't need to do anything fancy, they just need to be good people.

We have a young son, and we're talking about having another one, so we are pretty positive about our future. I have lots of plans, not enough money or time to get everything done right away, but we'll get it done when we can. I'm looking forward to my future—looking forward to spending time with my son and maybe my other children, and we'll see what happens.

All I Want Is Acceptance

Sergeant Marcus served in the U.S. Army from 1996 to 2004
as a multiple launch rocket system crewman.

I was in Iraq four years ago, when I was twenty-seven. I experienced ambushes, IEDs (improvised explosive devices), saw dead bodies and the evidence of casualties of innocents, and got news of fallen comrades. During traumatizing situations, I felt a very strong adrenaline rush and as if I were on autopilot. I reacted the way I had been trained to—most of the time without a second's thought: it was like a reflex. It felt like my heart was still pounding even hours after it was over. It was hard to sleep those nights. I can't remember much surrounding the events and afterwards. I think we tried to forget about it all and just go on.

Things didn't start to change until I was home for about three months: I felt like I had the impulse to really seriously hurt my son, who was two at the time. I thought my problems were more of a spiritual nature, so I talked to my chaplain. It was he who decided that I needed psychological counseling. I was diagnosed with PTSD in 2004 and was medically discharged from the army for PTSD under honorable conditions in July of the same year.

I wasn't happy anymore, when before I used to be. I lost the ability to "feel" anything. I have dysthymic disorder and suffer from depressive episodes. I lost interest in socializing, lost interest in almost everything. I became a recluse. I think I have a fear of people now; I have extreme trust issues and am always suspicious of others. Sometimes I think I'm paranoid. I can't relax, and I tend to walk away from people in the middle of a conversation. Not because of something they say—I think it's more that I don't realize they are still talking to me and think they are talking to someone else. It is kind of hard for me to grasp hidden meanings or understand phrases in conversations, and I have the tendency to say things that are not even part of the conversation. I also can't look people in the eye anymore when I talk to them.

I shy away from other soldiers for some reason—I think I feel guilty.

My behavior or speech is often inappropriate. I have intermittent explosive disorder and problems with anger and irritability. Most of the time I don't know what sets me off. I don't see it coming, and it's usually something insignificant that normally wouldn't matter. I also had physical PTSD-related outbursts towards other people but can't recall the exact details.

I'm suffering from extreme hypervigilance and anxiety and have panic and anxiety attacks with all the typical physical symptoms. They happen in crowded, hectic places or if something gets too far out of my understanding or control and I seize up.

My nightmares mostly are centered around the traumatic events in Iraq, but I also have many about incidents that never occurred. I often see the outcome that almost happened in the events but didn't. These are the hard ones because they still feel so real, and their realism confuses me: I feel like it really happened that way, and I wake up, not realizing that three years have passed and still thinking I'm in the dream.

I have intrusive thoughts and flashbacks, which are more or less erratic. Sometimes they are situational, but mostly they are general. My mind will wander, and all of a sudden I'm not here anymore but in the past. Highly stressful situations seem to provide the necessary ingredients to set a flashback off as well, just like triggers.

I avoid trash in the road even to this day as it reminds me of IEDs. When driving through construction areas on the highway, I really get uneasy because we had ambushes happen in that way. I can't drive with the windows down most of the time because it makes me feel insecure. I also don't like driving alone because sometimes I imagine I'm somewhere else. I get disoriented, and sometimes my eyes and imagination play tricks on me, especially at night. The way the lights appear in the rearview window freaks me out, and I feel like there is someone in the backseat that wasn't there before. Things moving in the shadows set me off as well.

Seeing war-related news—or news at all for that matter—is difficult for me. Bad news in general puts me in a bad mood, and then I am more prone to be hostile. I try to keep positive things in my mind because I'm terrified I will regress again.

I hate it when people look at me with pity or sorrow and sadness. I am the way I am, and they need not wish I were different. All I want is acceptance.

I want my family to understand that I still love them, and I don't want them to go away.

I go in cycles from bad to good, and I never really know what each day is going to be like. Medication has helped somewhat: recently I have been put on Cymbalta, and it has greatly improved my mood. I'm still having dreams and intrusive thoughts, but I feel better generally. My wife is very supportive, and some of my family are as well. I feel the therapy is a good release, and I look forward to each session for the ability to share.

I'm a disabled veteran and have accepted the concept of being home to see my children grow up. After going through Iraq, I feel very fortunate to even be here. I try not to let PTSD control what I do, but I realize that it is a part of me now and that I must not give up on life.

I Want People to Know That There Is Hope

Stephanie is married to Sergeant Marcus from the previous story.

It was about three months after my husband came back from Iraq that I realized something was wrong: he said he was having homicidal thoughts about people he worked with and bad thoughts that he may hurt his kids. He also started spending extra time on the computer: he would come home and immediately go to the computer and spend no time with me or the kids. He went from being a really affectionate man to one having no affection, from being able to hold a conversation to not being able to say anything, from holding eye contact to no eye contact, which at first I took as him not wanting to give me his whole attention. I asked him about this, and he said that he doesn't understand it himself, but we both know it's part of his PTSD. His memory has been affected as well, and he has a horrible time remembering what day it is or even the time at some points.

Marc's medical discharge from the army ended a successful eight-year active duty military career. He was seeing a psychologist while still in the service. As far as getting him to take medication, it seemed like I had to pull tooth and nail because he had had a bad experience before: they had him overmedicated while in the army—had him on Effexor, Klonopin, and Wellbutrin—and he used to be on the verge of passing out, overcome by sleep. You just couldn't talk to him, and he was like a zombie most of the time. It almost destroyed our marriage.

With the onset of PTSD, Marc found that he couldn't work anymore. He had tried to hold down two different jobs, but he stressed out so bad that he ended up in the emergency room for six hours with an intravenous drip in his arm because he broke out in hives and his throat closed up. He applied for Social Security disability and VA benefits.

When we first moved back here to Oklahoma City, a friend of ours had hooked him up with a job driving a tow truck. Marc was under a time crunch, and the pressure was mounting. He was downtown, and for a moment he was in the middle of some city in Iraq right before being ambushed. It was as if he vividly was remembering everything from before it happened and thus didn't know anymore where he was.

For a long time he would not drive over cans or trash in the road because, as he told me, that was what they would use to hide IEDs in Iraq.

Family life definitely changed for us. He went from a happy guy who enjoyed going places to always wanting to be home. He quit spending personal time with me and would escape into his video games. He was angry all the time, mainly with the kids. It was as if they couldn't do anything right, especially our oldest.

One time I also remember coming out of a Wal-Mart parking lot, and someone cut me off. Marc wanted me to follow that person home.

As far as social contacts go, he at first didn't care about the people he used to know. However, three years later, he has made efforts to be a bit more social to a few select ones. Concerning outings, he does not like crowds, and I respect that.

At first, the worst aspect of his PTSD was the lack of emotions he showed towards me and the kids. Now it is the fact that I know he will always struggle with PTSD. What's also very hard on us is not knowing how he will be from one day to the next.

I tried being supportive. In the beginning it was harder because emotions were so raw and everything was chaotic. I must admit at first I yelled a lot—I know that sounds awful. But understand that I wasn't just dealing with my husband having PTSD; I was dealing with eight previous years of being an overstressed, neglected army wife. I still feel resentment.

Then it was looking up information. When Marc was first diagnosed with PTSD, I wanted to know exactly what it was, how it was going to affect him, how it was going to affect me, and, most important, how it was going to affect our children.

I have been and am still learning to interpret Marc's body language, but I can usually tell what he is feeling. I always encouraged Marc to talk and still do. He did speak to me about his problems when he actually admitted them, and he knows that if he needs someone to listen, I am here for him. Sometimes I still have to gently press a little bit for information, but I feel it is helpful for him to talk to me so I know what's going on. In a strange way it helped that my father was a Vietnam veteran because I was and am better equipped to handle the things Marc tells me since my father was kind of graphic about his experience in the war.

I often joke that I have a big mouth, and I am not afraid to use it, meaning I wasn't afraid to tell Marc that some of the things he was doing, I wasn't going to just stand there and let him do them in the name of "He has problems, and I'm gonna be supportive." I lived that for seventeen years with my folks.

Marc's parents were understanding about his PTSD, but he and I both do not think they understood why he wasn't working. Marc's sister, whom he did not have the greatest relationship with before, pretty much stopped calling. She has never discussed it with him at all. Rather, she just keeps her interaction with him limited to once a year at Christmas, even though we attend the same church and she only lives ten minutes away. His extended family kept asking him, "Well, don't you want to do anything with your life?" We see those family members at Thanksgiving, and they do not call him. People at church treat us differently too. People he grew up with and whom he has known his whole life will hardly talk to him or expect him to be the same as before. Once in a while, someone he or I know will come up to him and ask what he is doing now. The reaction is always the same when he tells them he is a veteran and is now disabled: they either stop talking and walk away, or they look at him or me with pity in their eyes. The thing that bothers me the most is that church should be one of the places you can go to, where they accept you as you are, kind of like Christ would. We didn't isolate ourselves from everyone else; they actually alienated us. My side of the family was great. I am extremely close to my sister, who lives in Oregon. She was really understanding about the whole thing, never a doubt or question. She and Marc are close too, which helps a lot.

Marc and I have three children, ages four, six, and nine and a half. I don't think the two youngest will be as affected because they don't remember Daddy pre-PTSD. However, our oldest was five and remembers the deployment. She has come out with the fact that she has been afraid that her daddy is going to have to go back to Iraq. She even mentioned that he went to the war, and a different daddy came home. And it seems that much of his anger is directed towards her. She and I talk a lot about her dad. I try to encourage her to share her feelings with me. I tend to call it our "safe zone." It's the one place she can feel free to tell me what's on her mind and how she is feeling, and I'm not allowed to say a word. I just have to listen, unless she wants my advice. It helps her, I think. She has mentioned that Daddy isn't affectionate with her, Daddy doesn't play with her, Daddy doesn't talk to her, and she doesn't feel that she can talk to him. If she does want to share her feelings, most of the time I have to be there to start off the conversation because she is afraid that he will get mad at her. It breaks my heart, and I'm in tears talking about this. I never wanted that for my children. It brings my own childhood to mind.

I started with therapy after my husband was diagnosed with PTSD and have myself been diagnosed with secondary trauma from him being in Iraq and his issues. Of course I have my own triggers from growing up in a house with a Vietnam vet father. My father was never diagnosed with PTSD, and I didn't realize that he had it until my own husband was diagnosed with it. It's amazing how much I am learning about my deceased father through my husband. Some parallels that I see between them are mainly situational: the fact that I have no medical insurance and some of the financial problems we have had in the past. I learned when I was going to therapy for the first time that these were big issues for me because I also felt insecure when I was a kid and wasn't properly taken care of that way. There are also consequences concerning the treatment of the kids: I am especially protective of them, mainly because my mom never protected us from my dad. Then there is the irritability and those kind of things. I am working on both, those childhood memories—the abuse and neglect that resulted from my father's PTSD—and my current situation, and therapy has helped me tremendously to cope. There are also several other factors that have helped: one being the fact that Marc was willing to get help and, as of recent days, his willingness to get on medication. He just got put back on medication, and his symptoms within the past few weeks have been somewhat manageable. Another factor is that he is actually trying. He decided a while back that he wasn't going to just let PTSD control him.

It's so difficult thinking back three years ago sometimes. He and I have come a long way. Things have changed from his diagnosis till now, but I don't know if it was necessarily his symptoms or my willingness to try and understand what was going on with him or even him trying not to let the PTSD define who he was, what brought on the change.

I just want people to know that there is hope. Things can be better, but it takes not only the willingness of the spouse to be supportive but also the willingness of the vet to at least try. I am a firm believer in counseling and medication because they have helped myself and my spouse.

Marc and I have been married for over eleven years. Three years ago I left Marc because I couldn't handle any more stress. I was going to divorce him, and if you asked me three years ago why I came back, I would have told you it was because I had no other place to go. Now, I can say I am very blessed and happy that he and I stuck it out and to have the chance of learning to live with an entirely different person and allowing yourself to fall in love with him all over again.

It Was Always My Fault

Lana has been in the Canadian army for over fifteen years: twice as a reservist, twice as a regular force member, and once as a public service member. She was married to a Canadian soldier suffering from PTSD who has been serving for eighteen years in army communications as a signal operator and has five more years to go.

My former husband served in Iran/Iraq just before the war. He oversaw body exchanges, which became a "hot" trigger point for him. A body exchange is a set time and place where the dead of the other warring side are exchanged for the dead of your side so they can be buried. He also walked through a minefield once. After the minefield, he asked for a break. A friend of his took his next route and ran over a mine. His other tour was to Bosnia after it had calmed down, but he was with a unit he did not know, and isolation was a big factor for him: he had been abandoned by his mother as an eight-year-old child, who put him in foster care while keeping his six other siblings. Being alone is a very difficult thing for him to manage.

My husband left on that tour to Bosnia, and another person came back. I noticed that something was wrong the first night he arrived home. Separation for work was very normal for us—I joined the army when I was sixteen and am thirty-one now. This time, however, when he returned, he wasn't the same person at all: he was incredibly angry, irritable, and impatient. Just being near him, I could feel the overwhelming emotional tidal waves going on inside him. Still eight years later I haven't seen the man who left.

He operated well at work and let his anger escape when he got home. I let a lot of it go, thinking it would just take time to reintegrate this time: we had three very young children, so there were a lot of family demands that we weren't yet used to. At first, I thought it might just be this. Then there was an information session for spouses of members with PTSD on the base, so I got the time off work to attend. I recognized at this session that this was most likely the problem. When I suggested it to him, it was not well received (huge understatement).

I had to push as hard as I could to get him to go for help. It was exhausting. The few times I succeeded, which was about four times in four years, his options were to either get help or I was moving out with the kids. The last time I pressured him to seek help, he chose not to, so I left with the kids.

The first time he went to a doctor, he was told he was mildly depressed and to come back if it got worse. "Mildly depressed" was completely inaccurate, but this was before it was widely accepted that any military-related stress injury was valid, and he had seen a military doctor.

We requested a posting back to the city I was from to get extra family help with the kids. This meant I had to release from the military—that was the only way they would give my ex-husband the position. We moved and bought a farm, as it was the plan at that time to set up a berry farm as a retirement income. The new position wasn't working out for him, so he requested his release from the military. Thankfully, his request was reviewed by someone who recognized that something wasn't right. It was put on hold, and he was guided towards the medical side to get some assistance. He was referred to a civilian therapist, and I believe this is who diagnosed him with PTSD. The military was extremely helpful to him once it was recognized that he has PTSD. Although his work requirements did not change, he was given time off work whenever needed. There still, however, was nothing available to assist the family.

My ex-husband, quite strongly, did not want and accept help from me. He didn't believe he had a problem. I was the one with the problem, or the kids had the problem if they were doing something to make him mad. It was never him who had the problem. Even now, he believes a large part of the difficulties we had were my fault—that is, eight years after he became ill, and six years after being diagnosed with PTSD.

I tried to help but in hindsight likely only prevented him from getting better. Because the kids were one, two, and four and a half years, all their care fell into my hands, as well as working full-time. I was being a "single" parent with an angry, negative person always in the way. I would do whatever he wanted in an attempt to keep him happy, but nothing was ever enough to make it better. Trying everything I could to move the family around him to avoid conflict was not the best way to handle things, but I didn't know what to do.

Before leaving on his tour, he had a positive attitude. He was always thinking of new projects and ideas to try and then doing them. He was fun to be with, and he was very involved with the kids. Afterwards, he was always angry. He had no interest in anything, and he wouldn't interact with the kids—except to yell at them. There was nothing nice about him at all. Every attempt I made at trying to reconnect with him failed because he didn't want to talk—and every problem was in some way always my fault.

We lost all social contacts, and there was no time for hobbies: I couldn't leave the kids with him, and he never felt like going out, so that is how this pattern started. There was no opportunity to spend much time with friends. Family did not live near us, and the only neighbors we talked to were going through the same illness, with the same shadows and "don't ask, don't tell" atmosphere. So we didn't talk about it with them—it was very much in silence. My family and his didn't say much about it when we told them. It is very hard to understand PTSD unless you have lived through it.

My husband's disorder caused many disturbing situations before he was diagnosed and before we moved to be closer to my family:

I remember pleading with my two-year-old son to stop crying so his dad wouldn't get mad and lose his temper again. The problem wasn't my son—he was crying because his father had been mean to him.

I remember sitting on the floor in the living room, holding my son and daughter, who were then one and two years old. They were crying while their dad ran around the house, hitting the walls and yelling at us how it was all our fault.

I remember my husband being so mad at our four-year-old that he tried to step over the baby gate but knocked it down on top of our daughter, who was about two, and landed on the gate and her. His anger was irrational and out of control.

There was no mutual, caring intimate relationship left, and this, of course, was my fault. If I did not want to be intimate with him, then everyone suffered the next day with his terrible temper. Obviously this was very damaging, the extent of which I'm still learning about.

My ex-husband and I both served in the same trade; however, as a result of his PTSD, I switched to the Reserves and quit full-time military. I took a job with the reserve force and public service as a means to find a balance our family could survive at. It didn't work, and after the breakdown of our relationship, I rejoined the military full-time in a trade that deploys less.

We got a divorce after being married for five years, with four of those years suffering through the effects of PTSD. I had to leave with my children because I was simply living in survival mode. That was almost three years ago, and I still struggle with the wounds it has left on my children and me.

The constant tension and negativity were a great burden on the family. Being blamed for everything was hard, but the worst part was always wondering what would go wrong and when. It always did go wrong. There was never a sense of relaxation or peace. I noticed this most when I first got my own apartment with the kids. It was small, and the furniture was just pieced together; all was secondhand, and the TV on a box for a long time, but it was so peaceful that it seemed wonderful to me.

Meanwhile, my ex-husband is learning to control his behavior well, although he can't manage his feelings yet. He knows when he is going downhill—not quite quick enough yet, but at least he notices—and that is his signal to walk away and take a break. I have also taught the kids to watch for cues with him so they can tell when it is his sickness that is causing his behavior.

It is important for them to know that it is not always their fault when he yells. As far as I know, he still takes his medication. He went on another tour this past year and was sent home early because his PTSD was causing problems. Since his return in October 2006, he really cut me out of the picture—not sharing information, like things that do involve the kids, and generally just closing himself off again.

The divorce had been amicable until his return from this last tour. His reactions and expectations of me and the kids, following this tour, caused me to change how I "helped" him. He does have another girlfriend now who lives with him, so I expect her to help him. I have little contact with him. The oldest child, whom I adopted when I got married, has lived with him exclusively since 2004, but neither of them lets me know much about what goes on. Even after leaving the relationship, I continued to try to make things easier for him by making doctor's appointments etcetera for the oldest child, asking for the least amount for child support, so he could have more money, babysitting, so he could go on dates. . . . In the last five months, I have made an effort to change this. It has resulted in my stepson missing school and appointments and having more behavioral problems. On the other side, I am finally taking care of myself first. My new family is doing much better with my focus on us rather than trying to make my ex-husband's life easier. By not being available to him for help, he has had to change the way he is handling things. This is probably the right way of helping him. I want him to get better because the children still want to see him, and he doesn't handle things well yet with regards to them.

My ex-husband's PTSD has absolutely had a traumatizing effect on me. I have been in a new relationship for almost three years now. I worked with my current boyfriend before I met my husband and have known him for over ten years. Almost every time in the first year that we were intimate I would end up crying, sometimes just for a few minutes but sometimes for a long time. I'm just now starting to figure out why, with the counseling that I'm in. I was having anxiety attacks, which have stopped, thankfully. I panic very quickly whenever anything not good happens with my kids, which is exhausting and not necessary. I become overwhelmed by certain topics, so much that I can't function for hours or days: I have difficulties deciding what to make for supper, getting the motivation to make lunch for my kids; I don't want to talk to anyone, I can't read, or write. . . . It's like my brain just stalls, and it takes time before it will start going again.

The oldest child, now almost eleven years, has many behavioral problems. He is angry and sullen 90 percent of the time, he has trouble making and keeping friends, he is irresponsible and manipulative. He is not very loving or happy. He is quite rude to people in general but more specifically towards women. I got him into counseling. My other two children are delayed in reading, one is struggling in writing, one is struggling in math. Their personal coping skills regarding stress, responsibility, etcetera need improvement because of my overcompensation when living with their father. My son, seven years now, has problems with his anger. He is getting better but was having tantrums a lot. He has the tendency to try talking, but as soon as that doesn't work, he will hit. He is better now but still operating at about a five-year-old level for personal control of feelings. My daughter has problems with anxiety; she is eight years old. She will do extra work to prevent anyone from becoming upset rather than deal with them when they are upset. She will not tell her father about things that bother her if it will hurt his feelings. She will cover up for her older brother if he has done something to hurt her, either physically or emotionally, so that her dad doesn't get mad. She very strongly does not like when people yell.

If it's me having trouble coping, I tell my children that I got a little sickness from when I lived with their dad and that it affects me sometimes. I ask them to be more patient with me and to understand that until I'm feeling better, I might get angry easily, but I will try to take breaks so that it doesn't happen. If I take a break, I tell them I need a few minutes to myself and that it's important that they don't interrupt and give me the time I need to calm down. I just go lay down in my room and close the door. I am also in counseling now to try to learn new coping skills so I can unlearn some hurtful things from when we were together.

Although I had to end this relationship to regain a healthy life for me and my kids, I believe this was the only way I could manage. There was no help available to me or the kids when my husband was diagnosed, and as more help does become available, I am learning.

I was in poor health for a long time, but after changing a lot in my life, I have a stronger, healthier life now. My boyfriend and I have plans to get married and have a child together. It has taken this long, but life is finally good again.

My brother also served in Bosnia around 1994 and returned looking a lot older than he was when he left being twenty years old. He has found a healthy life now, but it took many years for him to recover also. He never was diagnosed.

Amongst my friends and coworkers in my previous trade, several have been diagnosed with PTSD as well.

It was all around me. I can see it from the side of a member, a spouse, an ex-spouse, a sister, and a friend. From all of this, I understand that good people get hurt and that there is a way to find some light in your life again. And it is very important to fight your way back to that light.

I Have Made
My Peace with It

*Former Acting Sublieutenant John joined the Canadian Re-
serves in 1982 and transferred into the regular force in 1983.
He went through the Regular Officer Training Program at
a civilian university until his graduation with a degree in
mechanical engineering in 1988 and served in Maritime Command (Navy) as a combat systems engineer. He was released
from the Canadian armed forces in 1990.*

On July 18, 1987, twenty years ago, I was involved in a near
collision between the replenishment ship USS *Milwaukee* and
the aircraft carrier USS *Forrestal* while conducting an underway
replenishment. I was a twenty-three-year-old Naval Cadet on exchange to the United States Navy on the "Midshipmen Exchange
Program," which let junior officers understand the operational
differences between the two navies. We were not officially trained
and, therefore, not supposed to take on any real responsibility.

The four midshipmen in the cycle before us, however, had complained that they were never able to do anything. So, the captain decided to let our group take real responsibility, and we were ordered to stand positions such as conning officer and helm safety, myself both. I asked what to do and was given a five-minute brief into a job that takes years to train for. After the officer I relieved had left, I turned to the enlisted man behind me and asked him if he could cover for me in case I made a mistake. All of the enlisted men around started to help me then. Unfortunately, one of these was the helmsman steering the ship. Twenty minutes later, while answering a question I had asked, he became confused and started turning the wheel the wrong way. Our helmsman was under instruction, but his instructor had left his post momentarily. We went way off course toward the carrier we were supposed to replenish. When the instructor returned, he pulled the trainee off the helm and corrected the problem.

However, at this point, we were already in too close. We called for an emergency breakaway. Not knowing what was going wrong, the carrier's captain ordered their helm to put over and then opened the throttles to leave. At the closest point, we were twenty feet apart at the hulls, five feet up top. The carrier turned hard away without releasing any of the lines and cables. These either snapped or were released under tension. Eighteen men were injured as they dove out of the way.

What I remember most when we were off course was the feeling when I believed we were going to kill people. That started in my feet, ran right up my body, and hit my brain so hard I thought it was going to blow my skullcap off. But then I thought, "Aw, fuck the dead! We're going to have wounded," and I began reviewing medical procedures.

People get irritated when they are almost killed. The two people they wanted to vent their anger on were the helmsman and helm safety. Everywhere I went there was someone offering their opinion. It was so bad that I actually tried to jump off the tanker and swim to the carrier. On my way to the side, I had a bowel cramp so severe it dropped me to the deck in agony. When it subsided, I shuffled over to a place to sit. I cried until the tension dropped. When it was low enough, I would decide to jump again. Then I would start to cry and the tension would drop. This kept going until one of the junior officers was instructed to take me to the wardroom. Once there, I started crying again. He said, "You fucked up, but you have to learn to live with it." Then I was taken to the executive officer's cabin. Once seated there, I started crying again. He said, "You fucked up! You really fucked up! But a real man will get over it."

And that was the moment it snapped. I know it was right then because I felt something change. After that, I stopped crying and would not cry again for months.

After PTSD was triggered, I had emotional numbing: I could not feel much. I had sailors coming up to me telling how they were almost killed, but I could not feel anything. They must have wanted to see if I cared, but I just listened until they were done and then went on. When USS *Milwaukee* returned to Norfolk, the families came on board the ship. I saw one officer who had nearly been killed by a snapping line hugging his two children while his wife rubbed his knee. Seeing that felt like a shotgun was put to my head and the trigger pulled. The pain started up front and then went right out the back before returning to the numbing feeling. Then it felt as if I was under a bright spotlight. I left before she could say anything.

I walked onto the main deck, where hundreds of sailors were hugging their wives and children. I immediately turned back inside and hid in my sleeping space. When they let people leave the ship, I walked around big fuel tanks near the dock because there was no one else there.

Shortly after leaving USS *Milwaukee* for a three-week stint on board USS *Biddle*, a guided missile cruiser, the numbness wore off over a space of three days: it was like standing on a railway track and hearing a train approaching. It got louder and louder until I was completely swept up. That is when the insomnia started. For the next few months, I never slept more than three hours a night.

My insomnia was curious, though. I would fall asleep between one and two in the morning and wake up between four and five after four in the morning. It became so routine that I would try to guess the minute I woke up and was correct on several occasions. I would also wake up immediately. It was like turning on a light. You are launched from sound sleep to wide awake. After that, it took a few seconds before the subconscious started cycling the memory of the event through my head again. In that period, I prepared for the bowel cramps.

These cramps did not happen every morning. When they did, I would roll over, clasp my pillow between my teeth, and scream. When the cramp subsided, I could place my hand on my abdomen and feel my intestines pulsing back and forth.

I was so weak from the lack of sleep that it took a while for my legs to be able to hold my weight. While on board *Biddle*, I hugged the post of the rack (bed) until they were strong enough. When I returned home, I would just crawl to the bathroom for a glass of water and then sit on the toilet for a while.

Shortly after I returned to Canada, my arms began shaking. When they shook while people were nearby, I would sit on my hands so they would not notice. I do not remember anyone ever mentioning anything about it.

An overwhelming emotion I felt was anger. I had never asked to go to the States, but my supervisor had talked me into putting it as my third choice for training that summer. I had tried telling the Americans that I fixed weapon systems, and they had not listened. I thought they were insane when I was ordered to stand conning officer. I had asked for instructions from the helm safety officer when I replaced him and had even asked for help from the enlisted personnel. What else could I have done to prevent this?

For two weeks I had taken it from the crew. The day of the "JAG" (Judge Advocate General's Corps' investigation) was to be the day when reason returned. I expected the investigating officer would place his hand on my shoulder and tell everyone I was not to blame. That did not happen. He asked if we were on course before we had called the breakaway, and we affirmed this. Then he turned to me and said, "So, if you had kept the captain informed, we would have avoided that whole breakaway."

I no longer wonder what it feels like to swallow a watermelon whole. I was expecting to be acquitted, but instead it turned out that I was to blame. That thought went in and would stay hidden for months. The memory was blocked.

This was another symptom that many of the events were blocked from my memory. In fact, I could not remember during the investigation what had happened while we were on course. I remembered the point up to just before the helmsman called out, "Helm is not responding!" The next memory was seeing the carrier some distance away after I had been relieved. Every answer I gave during the investigation was what I had thought had happened. I could not remember it. The investigation would also be blocked from my memory.

The memories slowly returned. One of the first was, "Aw, fuck the dead!" That one hurt because I could not see how I could be so cold to the ones who would have died. I had not been able to face their families, and now I seemed to be willing to toss their memories aside. A few days later, the second half of the thought emerged: "We're going to have wounded." Then the statement made sense. Any dead would have to wait until the wounded were tended to.

Another blocked memory was the suicide attempt by one of the sailors: He had cut his wrists. That memory came out at the beginning of an exam. I turned my wrists down so I could not see them and subsequently failed the exam. For the next few months, every time I saw my wrists, I would wonder what extra stress it would take for me to cut my wrists. That was a thought I did not want to deal with, so I avoided looking at my wrists. This means you have to make sure your eyes are tightly closed while shampooing. You have to look away while shaving, and your arms must be twisted so the wrists lie flat while studying.

The final memory block was the investigation. This memory was not released until after I learned what happened in the investigation: the helmsman under instruction had tested positive for drug abuse and was discharged from the navy.

My initial response was to be overjoyed that I had not been blamed. That soon changed back to anger, and I did not know why, until the last memory popped out: when the investigator's comment came out, it literally knocked me off my feet. I landed on my hands and knees and started pounding the ground in anger. It was not a fair comment, and I was not able to defend myself against it.

Initially there were also periods where I entered a "dissociative state" whereby I would be walking and then would emerge from the state some time later and a long distance away from where I last remembered being. I had crossed busy highways without getting hit. After doing this several times, I assumed that I had stopped at the light, pushed the walk button, waited for the proper time to cross, and that I was simply on autopilot at the time.

Emotional hypersensitivity was another symptom. Emotions would instantaneously go from nothing to the maximum amount that could be felt. Every emotion was felt so strongly that it hurt. To avoid the pain, most PTSD sufferers avoid all contact with others, leading to antisocial behavior. Unfortunately, I tended to be the opposite. I felt that this situation was not my problem, and I was not going to be the only one to deal with it. So I talked with anyone who would listen and a whole bunch of people who would not. Of course, I only told the part about the near collision and not about being trapped on board a ship with sailors coming up telling how they were almost decapitated. In the end, a lot of people became antisocial towards me: I talked about it so much that they avoided me.

I also was suffering from hyperarousal. If someone was late, I immediately assumed they were dead. This lead to the annoying "don't move anything" syndrome: when something changed around me, I had to examine all possible outcomes of the change to ensure it would not come back to hurt me. As long as things did not change, I could relax. The moment they would change, I would panic.

When I began having panic attacks, I had no idea what they were. Since it felt like I was drowning, I thought my mind was trying to scare me by showing what it would have felt like if I had drowned. So, I ignored the sensation. After several of these attacks, I found that they were usually triggered by an additional stress, such as walking into a hot building while having my parka zipped up tightly. Each time they occurred, I would find the source of the trigger and remove it. Then I would calm my breathing and move about until the sensation passed.

Though I hated having panic attacks, there seemed little to do but endure them. Eventually I got so used to dealing with them that the response was conditioned in. Initially I had to do this at a conscious level. Now, when I feel the start of an anxiety attack, I wait to see if I have to do anything at the conscious level, but I can feel the subconscious stopping the attack all by itself.

I also had to deal with the memory of the event constantly cycling through my brain. It started about ten seconds after I woke up and continued until I finally fell asleep. It was like having a set of headphones strapped to my head, constantly replaying the same song over and over again at a volume so loud I could not hear myself think. There was no arguing with it, and there was no bargaining with it. For the first six months, it never, ever stopped.

On December 20, 1987, the tanker *Vector* collided with the ferry *Dona Paz* off of the Philippines. The collision killed over 2,000 people. In a horrid case of déjà vu, the eventual cause turned out to be that untrained people were left at the helm of the tanker. USS *Milwaukee* was carrying seventeen times as much fuel as the *Vector* along with hundreds of tons of ammunition.

It would seem rather ironic that a major disaster would make me feel better. However, the collision did just that: the event took my attention from my incident at a conscious level and allowed my subconscious to complete its task. I focused on any news I could catch from the papers. About four weeks after the collision, the memory stopped cycling through my brain.

When I was involved in the near collision I knew at that time that I needed help right away. My incident was so powerful that it seemed natural that I would have problems with it. On the second American ship I was on, I paced in front of the padre's cabin because I was having so much difficulty dealing with it. Out of fear of another snapback, I could not ask for assistance from him. So I waited until I returned to Canada: within twelve hours, I was on the phone with my supervisor. His intent was solely based on protecting my career, and he did not give any information on how to proceed with psychological assistance, just recommended seeing a doctor for the medical problems, such as abdominal pains.

I hoped to be able to help myself by "putting my head down and trying to charge right through it." This was mad. It caused several bouts of the dissociative state. It also triggered a return to the "void" of emotional numbing. If I pushed hard enough, I could make the pain go away. I called this "powering down." As the months wore on, this did not work anymore. When I pushed, it would not return to the void. I just received more pain.

Eventually, I could not take it anymore and went to the pastor of my church for help. He sent me to a counselor who told me that this was all normal. I was not going crazy.

After that meeting, I stopped fighting it. I accepted the pain. This allowed my sleep to rise, and I began to feel better.

The following spring I passed my last year of engineering and was sent to the Canadian naval base in British Columbia to continue my training. Since I had been in a civilian university, no one knew about my condition. Now that I was back in the military full-time, I started having problems. At the subconscious level, returning to sea for me had become tantamount to suicide. Having been stuck on a ship that was 659 feet long and 96 feet wide, there was no way to get 660 feet away from everyone. I had very nearly thrown myself off the side of the tanker just to get away from the other sailors. At the conscious level, I wanted to charge through and give it a try.

Many people like to give the old speech about conquering your fears: I should have conquered my fear and defeated it. When I say that I could not go back to sea, this statement should not be dismissed as a coward not willing to try. I fought as hard as I could fight, but it was no use. Accepting that I could not return to sea was not easy.

I could push no further, and I asked for help. I have never refused psychiatric assistance or been embarrassed that I would need it. A commanding officer in my Training Review Board recommended me for long-term psychiatric assistance. I was excited with that because I wanted to figure out what was wrong. They sent me to the psychiatrist to find the problem, and he claimed I hated my father. He said there was nothing more he could do for me.

About nine months later, I finally sorted out my problems: I had followed an order that had nearly killed 5,000 people. I could not follow orders anymore. Being forced to do so was causing too much stress, so I asked for a release from the Canadian armed forces.

For more psychological assistance, I was sent to the new psychiatrist, who supported my request for release, but to no avail. A third psychiatrist agreed with the second one, though, and the first one then signed off on it as well.

After lots of difficulties and a long, draining battle, I was finally discharged from the Canadian armed forces.

After my release, I worked for a small defense contractor for a while. The company owner reminded me of the tanker's captain, and I found myself shouting at him on occasion. Eventually I was fired, but it was time to move on anyway.

I have never returned to sea or had a desire to. I do not know what it would be like if I had to. PTSD has left me with a paranoia of going to sea, but since I am quite firmly landlocked where I live now, there is no need to treat it. So, I simply accept that I cannot return to sea and do not endlessly torture myself because I refused to conquer the mountain. I do not regret the decision for a moment. Even years later, I still believe it was the right thing to do.

Perhaps the one situation that was the most difficult to deal with was trying to meet the expectations of others. I could not be the same as before, no matter how many "magic words" were spoken. People tried to cure me be telling me some inane truth that they thought would immediately fix everything. When it did not help, they thought I was not trying. My friends and family were helpful when they listened to what I had to say. They were not helpful when they pushed for me to be healed immediately. You need time to heal, and it is difficult if people are not willing to give it to you.

A year or so after my release, I realized that I was blaming every single problem in my life on the incident. I had to train myself not to do that. I just had to live with the memories and not let them control my life.

What has not changed, perhaps because I do not want it to, is my anger at how PTSD sufferers are treated. If you have a medical problem, the world opens its arms in comfort. If you have a mental problem, people line up to kick you in the ass. It was so brutal at the Naval Officer Training Center that one of the trainees who had cancer said she felt sorry for me. People understood her pain and left her alone. She could not even comprehend what it was like for me; still, they were laughing behind my back and calling me a coward.

This is not only limited to the military. I found out that people were tired of my pain at my church. Now, every time I sit in a church, I get a headache. So, I just don't go.

The memory of the event no longer cycles through my mind, and I go about my life much like before. I guess this is something for people enduring PTSD to strive for. There is still an underlying anger at what happened, but it does not haunt me everyday.

I know what happened and have made my peace with it. If I am forced to review the memories, tears will still flow. This shows that I am still human and have not hardened myself so severely that I cannot feel anything.

People whom I meet now would never suspect I have been through PTSD. I always joke around and am quick to make others laugh. It is hard for them to believe that, for a while, I did not laugh at all. But people who have had PTSD can learn to laugh again. When people ask if I am back to normal, I reply that I am back to my usual state of abnormality. I guess I just learned to deal with the effects so efficiently that they no longer bother me. I have never believed that life is fair. You simply have to play the hand you are dealt and do the best you can with it.

I was barely passing engineering when I went through PTSD, and my self-esteem was pretty low. Having gone through it and sorted out my own problems, I feel much better about myself. I know that whatever happens, I can sort out the problem and carry on.

Scars and Memories Will Remain in My Soul

Friedhelm has been serving in the German army since 1992. He is specialized in electronic combat.

On June 7, 2003, I was a victim of the suicide attack on the bus of the ISAF in Kabul, Afghanistan, at the age of thirty-two.

The bus was on the way to the airport, from where we were going to be sent back to Germany. It all happened so damn fast. At first I believed we had run over a gigantic curb, then I thought of the detonation of a mine. But when the fog in the bus had settled and I awoke from something like a doze, I knew that more must have happened. At first I thought I was going to die, jammed between some chairs. I couldn't see anything, hear anything, or taste anything. I was almost like paralyzed, but then I functioned like a robot. Flight was my first impulse. But was that really me having this thought? If I had taken flight, I would have deserted my comrades, and that I could have never forgiven myself for. At that moment, however, I was selfish and thought only about myself and my family.

I was standing in the street. It was still empty of people, but there was blood everywhere and severed body parts, and it was unbearably hot. I had the feeling that I needed to take the next bus and go home. But there was no next bus. Time seemed to stand still. At first, nothing happened, and then suddenly, I was surrounded by numerous rescue workers. I can remember well how the platoon leader of the transport-security, who was standing next to me, was shouting through his megaphone, "Get all the rescue workers you can!" Then I found myself next to one of my comrades. An emergency doctor handed me a transfusion, and I was supposed to hold it while she tried to save the body that was lying there. The infusion led nowhere. Still, I kept holding it as if it would make sense. The comrade was dead.

I turned into a machine. I had no feelings anymore. I was indifferent and tried to avoid contact with the outside world as much as I could. I simply felt empty and didn't know if I should laugh or cry or what else. I took in what was happening around me, but often it didn't even touch me. The images of the attack that I was constantly seeing in my mind left me almost emotionally numb. Sometimes I wished I had been unconscious; then I wouldn't have had all those images.

On the other hand, I sometimes started to cry for no reason: when I was looking for the causes, there were none. What had been near and dear to me suddenly seemed strange and frightening. I considered help to be annoying and rejected it most of the time. "Bad devil" seemed to have me tightly in his grip. For the first time in my life, I didn't know whether I was coming or going. In moments like these, I remembered the question that was put to us during an officer's training course: "Where is the soul?" I made myself believe that I didn't have a soul anymore and couldn't even find an explanation as to how I came to this theory. I wanted to cry because I felt like it but had no tears; I wanted to laugh because that's what I always did when I felt like it, but I couldn't. Before, I had always laughed wholeheartedly, but now, this didn't work anymore. When I felt close to tears, I only wanted to be with the guys—all those from my unit who were on the bus with me, although four are no longer with us. Now I wanted to see the images, to be alone with them. I was no longer able to express my feelings in a way that others would understand them. I only wanted to be alone.

I also couldn't sleep well in the beginning, but I got it under control somehow.

I have a strong feeling for justice. It was not the case that I changed positions that time, but suddenly, I couldn't have cared less who did what, when and how, and whether it was right or wrong. Good wasn't necessarily good and bad not necessarily evil. This was especially true with the people that had meant a lot, if not everything, to me before. I didn't care how they felt, what they did and why. I didn't value affection enough, maybe even took it the wrong way.

I submerged myself in work. I couldn't get enough of it and felt that it gave me a higher quality of life. Only far too late did I realize that not only my marriage but also my social environment suffered from of it. Hobbies and social contacts didn't count anymore. Why should they? Things went along very well without them, at least during that time. You don't realize what is important, who is important, what's fun, what's good for you. The only thing I always tried was to build an especially close relationship with my then six-year-old son. I had the feeling of having done something wrong, that I wanted to do everything different now, to be a role model, or to show that something like that would never happen again. Till now I don't know whether I have been able to accomplish this.

After the attack, I started getting terribly upset about the smallest little things that would have left me cold before. I became easily irritable, and, at times, I wasn't even sure if that was really me. Certain key words, like June 7, attack, bus, Afghanistan, or Kabul, brought me into the arena right away. It seemed as if my soul was completely out of balance.

Sometimes I recalled images in my mind, to better understand one thing or the other and the question as to why.

There were several everyday situations which instantaneously reminded me of the seconds during the attack that had seemed like hours to me. It was especially difficult for me to go jogging along my favorite stretch in a beautiful, dense timber forest, like in the old days. Every time I approached a certain location or often already several yards before, this specific "movie" went through my mind—even though neither fauna nor flora nor anything else fit in the picture. Why then did I and do I still have this scene in my head? That's what I'm still asking myself today. I'm still afraid to go there since in that moment I always try to fade out pictures that aren't even there. But because of my fear of having to remember again at this spot in the forest, I force myself to go there, to find an explanation. Why I'm doing this in a particular moment seems rather paradoxical, but I can't steer it.

Crowds bothered me, and I avoided them whenever I could.

I absolutely evaded every question that might have been leading to the suicide attack. To get the attention away from me was the most important thing. I think I've always managed that pretty well. I felt uncomfortable when I had the feeling that all of the world was looking at me, expecting answers that I often did not have. I also wanted to prevent falling prey to hypocrisy.

I believe that I have suppressed a lot. I actually became calmer and more balanced—at least that's what I felt. I told myself that things were working out fine. But I hadn't reckoned with my soul.

In the end, I found myself in a vicious circle. There were several short trials at the neurological and psychiatric departments in the hospital, which scared me more than anything else. The first time, I was put in a four-bed room in a locked ward. I didn't mind the four beds but couldn't take being locked in. I wasn't sick, so why was I then in a ward for patients with alcohol and drug addictions and other problems? I couldn't place any trust into the therapy and quit after a few days. My troop physician showed a lot of empathy and understanding for this and referred me to a civilian psychologist. I had the impression that nobody knew how to help me. About seven or eight months after the attack, another doctor sent me, despite my skepticism, to yet another trauma specialist at one of the military hospitals. I didn't want to give up, especially not myself! But this was exactly where I was heading for; however, I didn't want to accept it. The trauma specialist turned out to be key to a successful treatment. I quickly trusted him. He used Davanloo's Intensive Short-term Dynamic Psychotherapy. This highly intensive conversational therapy was at first very exhausting and burdening and reminded me of an interrogation: The therapist tried to make me open up. More and more I felt that I wanted to speak about things I had kept hidden before. It was as if a load was being taken off me and I was able to breathe freely again. Within a week, I was back on track.

I never wanted to talk about my PTSD, as others might have thought of me as being "unstable," "not cut out for the job," or something similar. I wanted to avoid that. My family were the first to notice the change in my behavior and to suffer from it. I have never been able to tell my wife what was going on inside of me. I've also never really told her how important she was for me, how much she helped me during those hard times, without ever reproaching me for anything. I greatly respect her and the kids for this.

My PTSD had no consequences on my career in the military. The unit I belonged to was interested in seeing that I get well.

I was deployed again in 2007. Naturally, I gave it a lot of intensive thought whether I should go again or not. I actually had to convince my superiors that I want to and can. I had discussed it with my family beforehand in great length. Already a short time after the attack I knew that I wanted to go back to my profession. I was deployed again from March till June 2007, with the same company, in the same function, only with other people. It was a good feeling to be one of them again.

There are things in life that cannot really be influenced. One tries to sugarcoat them by calling them fate. But there are also things that don't help you much. I didn't "grow" because of the trauma.

Almost six years have passed since the attack. I guess I have learned to cope with this day, June 7. I'll never forget and also don't want to forget. Scars and memories will remain in my soul. I have not only lost comrades but also friends because of an insane action. I wish their families and all of us the necessary distance to be able to function again in daily life. We have become a "small community," something like a family. I'm glad about that.

The images, the event, have become part of my life. Nevertheless, I feel that I'm able to continue in my profession and my life normally again. What also helps me is that I've identified myself completely with being a soldier and still like my job.

I know it is hard to admit to oneself that one is in a state of psychological imbalance. It almost seems like an insurmountable barrier to go see a doctor or a psychologist, but it's the only sensible way. One's social environment, one's family are most of the time the driving force. You don't only suffer yourself, but there is the danger of pulling the others into the boat as well. That's not only unfair but also wrong. We have the possibility to get help, and we should do so.

You Think You Are the Only One

Sergeant Pierre served in the Canadian army from 1980 to 1994. He was an armor troop sergeant with the 12th RBC (Régiment blindé du Canada).

I was thirty years old when we deployed to Srebrenica, Bosnia, in 1993/1994. I cannot accept the fact that people died and we weren't able to do anything to protect them. They died in front of me. I felt horrible and asked myself why we don't have the power to do anything. The worst is that I feel as if I were the killer.

I lost my self-confidence and stopped believing in myself. I also constantly panicked during conversations, and afterwards I always felt guilty. I did not sleep well and drank to forget my bad nights. I cried all the time when I was alone.

I had been a good hockey player, a golf player, and an alpine ski instructor, and I lost interest in all of that. I stopped skiing, I stopped playing hockey, I stopped playing golf—I stopped doing everything I liked. I built up walls around me, stopped seeing my friends. I just wanted to be alone, by myself. That was bad.

I often had problems with driving because I was not able to concentrate on the road, and I was very aggressive. If somebody cut me or swore at me, I always jumped out of my car and ran after that person. My behavior was dangerous. I was terrible and stupid, but I was not a mean person—I was just not myself.

I attempted suicide twice, and after that, I had several flashbacks, a lot of anger and frustration.

When you come back after a mission like that, you never will be the same person again. You look at things differently, and don't do things the same as before anymore.

After I returned from that deployment, I slept only two hours a night. The day isn't long enough for me anymore. I am hyperactive and have to move all the time, have to stay busy all the time. I want to do everything at once—to me, to sit down and read a book, is to lose time. I can't just sit on my couch or go outside and have fun in my pool. To sleep seems stupid to me because you should be doing something—life's too short. Before that, I was relaxed and the type of guy who thinks, "Why do things now if you can do them later?" But now it's, "Do everything right away because you don't know what's going to happen tomorrow." So I try to do everything in one day, just in case I am not here anymore tomorrow—you never know. I'm definitely not the same as I was.

I broke off two relationships and said to my girlfriends, "You have a problem"—it was never my fault. One day I was told that I have PTSD and that *I* have a problem, not the others—*I* have the problem. That gave me a big shot in my face—that's a Quebecer expression—but it made me realize that it was my fault, not that of the others. I was really shocked about it because I had caused a lot of emotional pain. My behavior towards my last three girlfriends was not okay. I did not hurt them physically but verbally. I also always kept everything inside. When they asked me, "What's going on, why are you crying?" I always replied, "You piss me off, go away." I didn't want to talk with them.

I sought professional help for the first time ten years after my traumatic experiences:

Within two years after returning from my deployment, I had left eight jobs, and I had so many problems since I was fighting with people all the time. After about two years, I had told myself, that's the way I am, and if they don't like me, then that's the way it is. In 2004 I had a big verbal fight with my director in my last job. That time I was crying, and I came home and felt terrible. My friend, who was in the army too, came to my house. He had heard about the program OSISS (Operational Stress Injury Social Support) in Canada and suggested that I contact them. I talked with my girlfriend, and the day following that fight, I phoned VA Canada. I told them that I needed help because I felt like that time when I tried to kill myself: I had hung myself, but the rope broke, and I woke up the next day on the floor with the rope around my neck. I felt as if I was going to do something like this again, so the VA sent me to a psychologist, who referred me to a specialist for PTSD. There I was evaluated for three hours, during which I had to answer at least 400 questions. Afterwards they informed me that I am suffering from severe PTSD, and I started with therapy. At that time, I saw somebody who was working for OSISS, and I asked her if I am the only one: you always feel that you are the only one, and that's why you don't seek help. She answered that I'm not alone.

My current girlfriend told me that she was going to help me get through whatever problem I have and that she would be with me all the time. That helped me a lot.

I did not know my girlfriend at the time I was traumatized in Bosnia, so when I started with my therapy, she wanted to understand what's happening. I joined OSISS in Montreal and took a course with them. I didn't know how to explain to my girlfriend and my son, who is twenty-two years old now, what I was feeling and why I'm feeling like this, so I brought them to the briefing with the group in Montreal. This was my way to demonstrate to them which problem I had. They came to see me at the end, gave me a hug and thanked me. That felt good.

My girlfriend has two daughters. Now things are okay, but at first it was hard with the kids for me, as they are not mine, and they are thirteen and fifteen years old: in Bosnia we couldn't trust any kids because they had grenades, and they didn't have any respect.

All my friends and my family know about my PTSD and give me social support. When I get triggered, I still panic very easily, for example, when talking about particular things. Sometimes I swear and argue, and I quickly get into a bad mood. When this happened, my friends who had come to see me turned everything into a joke to get me out of my panic mode and bring me back into the conversation. That was good. When I realized that, I felt guilty and said to myself in my mind, "God damn it, what's happening, what did you do?!"

The doctor gave me pills to relax and to sleep, but the pills for relaxation made me put on a lot of weight. I also didn't work out anymore and got a big beer belly, which pissed me off. So I tried to stop the pills, but that was not a good idea. I started taking them again, started doing physical training, and changed my eating habits. Now I work out every day and lost a lot of weight again. I feel better, both in mind and body. That has helped me a lot. I started doing some of the things I did before, and I bought a motorbike. Together with some friends I took lots of trips around Canada and the United States on our motorbikes during summer, which was great.

With the treatment and the pills, the problems aren't that big. You still have the problem, and the symptoms are still there, but in my therapy, they show you how to live with them. And that's the important thing: how to live with PTSD and accept the situation.

Before our deployment that time, we were training for combat operations, and when we went over there, they told us things had changed: "You won't shoot, you won't do anything, you'll watch people die—it's not your war." That's the worst thing, the problem all the guys have. So in my therapy, they taught us how to cope when you aren't feeling good.

For many of us Christmas is a bad time because all the missions we did were during the holiday season. We saw a lot of people die, we saw a lot of dead bodies, people without food, without a house. I was in so much emotional pain over there. Every year during Christmas in Canada, my fellow soldiers and I think about that, and we feel very sad; I feel like crying all the time and don't enjoy Christmas. But with the help of my therapy, it was not too bad this year: a couple of days before Christmas, I was depressed, but only a bit, and on Christmas Day I felt good. Between Christmas and New Year I did pretty well, and New Year's Eve was excellent. It was my first year since 1994 that I had fun.

Twelve years have passed since that deployment.

I'm still in therapy at the hospital and see my therapist and my doctor every two weeks. I still have some nightmares and flashbacks, but they are not as bad anymore and less frequent. My psychologist is very good and makes me understand a lot of things. I still take some medication and will need to continue for a while. But I'm getting a lot better. I hope to be able to reduce my sessions from twice a month to once a month or even once every two months.

I'm working full-time for OSISS now as a peer support coordinator and am part of the mental health team: I'm there to help all the army guys with operational stress injuries—and that has helped me a lot in return.

The military people that come back from Afghanistan stop in Cyprus for a week, and during that week we give them a briefing about operational stress injury, a lecture on anger management, and we tell them where they can get assistance if they need help. Many soldiers talk to me about their experiences; they talk about bad things that happened to them, and I'm their confidant. It's a big trigger for me, and when I return, I need to talk to my therapist to get all of that out of my mind again.

Seeing war-related news is difficult for me as well. It affects me deeply inside and makes me suffer.

A lot of people, my family and friends, told me that they are proud of what I did and of what I am doing with my job.

I've formed two groups at OSISS, and every other Wednesday, we get together and talk about all kinds of things, about what's going on in each other's lives, but not about negative things. We joke and have a good friendship, and when I need to talk, they're right there.

My family thinks it's great that I like my job. They said, "We can see in your face that you are happy; we can see in your eyes that you're feeling fine." I felt really good when they told me that.

My goal for the future is to get better and to become a "better person," not to feel guilty anymore, to be calmer and relaxed. The first step to reaching that stage is that I have to accept my situation. I'm almost there.

My challenge is to help as many people as I can with this problem. I always say, somebody helped me, I have to help somebody else, my fellow men. When somebody does something good for you, you turn around, and you do something good too. We have so many guys that kill themselves. I want to make it clear to them that they should not commit suicide and that the best way to deal with your life is to deal with your problem. In order to reach my goal, I have to be in good health and enjoy doing my job. Because if you don't, you cannot do it well.

Glossary

List of terms that are not explained in Part I.

Agoraphobia   Phobic anxiety disorder, including fears of public places, crowds, shops, and so on, and, in extreme cases, of leaving home

Cymbalta   Trade name for duloxetine, an antidepressant for the treatment of major depression and generalized anxiety disorder

Davanloo's Intensive Short-term Dynamic Psychotherapy   Developed by Habib Davanloo, a psychiatrist and psychoanalyst; aims at overcoming internal resistance to experiencing true feelings that have been warded off because they are too frightening or painful

Dysthymic disorder   Chronic low-grade depression

Effexor   Trade name for venlafaxine, an antidepressant for the treatment of major depression and panic and anxiety disorders

Fluoxetine   Trade name Prozac: antidepressant for the treatment of major depression, panic disorder, and PTSD

IED   Improvised explosive device

Intermittent explosive disorder   Impulse control disorder, with extreme expressions of anger

Klonopin   Trade name for clonazepam, an anticonvulsant and muscle relaxant also used for the treatment of panic and anxiety disorders

Lexapro   Trade name for escitalopram, an antidepressant for the treatment of major depression and panic and anxiety disorders

NBC   Nuclear biological chemical

NyQuil   Cold medicine

Paxil   Trade name for paroxetine, an antidepressant for the treatment of major depression, PTSD, and panic and anxiety disorders

Remergil   Trade name for mirtazapine, an antidepressant for the treatment of depression, PTSD, and panic and anxiety disorders

Tet Offensive   A series of operative offenses of the forces of
the National Liberation Front for South Vietnam (NLF or
Vietcong) and the People's Army of Vietnam (the North Vietnamese army) against the forces of the Republic of Vietnam
(South Vietnam), the United States, and their allies in 1968
during the Vietnam War

Welbutrin/Wellbutrin   Trade name for bupropion, an antidepressant for the treatment of depression and anxiety disorders

Zoloft   Trade name for sertraline, an antidepressant for the
treatment of major depression, PTSD, social anxiety, and
panic disorder

$$\mathcal{R}ecommended\ \mathcal{R}eading\ \mathcal{L}ist$$

The following books are suitable for all readers:

After the War Zone: A Practical Guide for Returning Troops and Their Families
Matthew J. Friedman, PhD, MD, Laurie B. Slone, PhD
Da Capo Press, 2008
This book offers troops and their families resources and strategies for the transition between war zone and home and for reintegration into daily life and reconnecting with family and provides information on how to deal with common aftereffects of deployments, including anger, guilt, moral dilemmas, PTSD, and other mental health problems.

Soldier's Heart: Survivors' Views of Combat Trauma
Edited by Sarah Hansel, PhD; Ann Steidle, RN; Grace Zaczek, MPH; and Ron Zaczek, Veteran, USMC
Sidran Press, 1995

A compilation of original prose, poetry, and art by veterans, dealing with various emotions while suffering and healing from PTSD.

An Operators Manual for Combat PTSD: Essays for Coping
Ashley Hart II, PhD
iUniverse, 2000
This book offers help on how to monitor triggers and find a harmonic balance between the world within the veteran and the world we live in, in order to be able to cope with everyday life and develop an essential well-being.

Back from the Front: Combat Trauma, Love, and the Family
Aphrodite Matsakis, PhD
Sidran Press, 2007
This book wants to give a better understanding of combat trauma and its possible effects on family life, providing resources, coping strategies, and information on depression, PTSD, emotional numbing, sexual difficulties, anger, guilt, family violence, and other problems. It also shows the many ways in which a veteran's experiences can help enrich the family.

Vietnam Wives: Facing the Challenges of Life with Veterans Suffering Post-Traumatic Stress. 2nd ed.
Aphrodite Matsakis, PhD
Sidran Press, 1996
Intended primarily for wives of veterans, this book is also helpful to extended family and close friends who want to learn about the causes, symptoms, and effects of PTSD and how to recover from it. It shows better ways of how traumatized veterans and their families can cope with midlife challenges like retirement, the "empty-nest syndrome," becoming grandparents, and also divorce.

The Body Remembers: The Psychophysiology of Trauma and Trauma Treatment
Babette Rothschild, MSW, LCSW
W. W. Norton, 2000
This book explains the effects of trauma on mind and body in an easily understandable way and describes psychotherapeutic techniques.

The Post-Traumatic Stress Disorder Sourcebook: A Guide to Healing, Recovery, and Growth. 2nd ed.
Glenn Schiraldi, PhD
McGraw-Hill, 2009
This book describes many treatment strategies, alternatives, and self-management techniques that are helpful to trauma survivors, including war veterans and substance addicts, and shows that recovery and growth is possible.

The PTSD Workbook: Simple, Effective Techniques for Overcoming Traumatic Stress Symptoms
Mary Beth Williams, PhD, LCSW, CTS, and Soili Poijula, PhD
New Harbinger Publications, 2002
This book offers exercises, techniques, and interventions to conquer physical, mental, and emotional PTSD and Complex PTSD symptoms.

Acknowledgments

My heartfelt thanks go out to the following:

My interview partners, for their trust in me, their willingness to share their stories, and for taking the time to answer my questions.

Harold Kudler, MD, associate clinical professor, for providing a foreword.

Priv.-Doz. Martin Sack, MD, for his technical advice.

Norbert Kröger, PhD, for his technical advice and for putting me in touch with an interview partner. Heinz Sonnenstrahl, Captain (ret.); Peter Zimmermann, MD; Jared Ellis; Sandra Guenther; and Jennifer Fairbank for helping me find interview partners.

Professor Charles R. Figley, PhD, and Professor Kathryn M. Magruder, MPH, PhD, for their endorsements. Thanks also to all future endorsers.

My agent Claire Gerus for her enthusiasm and hard work.

Suzanne I. Staszak-Silva, Melissa McNitt, and the team at Rowman & Littlefield for their hard work.

In addition, I'd like to thank every other person who has been of any help along the way.

About the Author

Leah Wizelman is a German American biologist, currently doing research at the Technical University of Munich, Germany, on psychophysiological aspects (mechanisms of stress regulation) of posttraumatic stress disorder. She holds the German university degree "Diplom" in biology and is working on her doctorate.